Re-Creative

Re-Creative

50 projects for turning found items into contemporary design

Steve Dodds

KEY PORTER  BOOKS

Conceived and produced by
Elwin Street Limited
144 Liverpool Road
London N1 1LA
www.elwinstreet.com

Library and Archives Canada Cataloguing in Publication

Dodds, Steve

      Re-Creative: 50 projects for turning found items into contemporary design / Steve Dodds.

ISBN 978-1-55263-914-6

      1. Found objects (Art). 2. Found objects (Art) in interior decoration. 3. Handicraft.

4. House Furnishings. I. Title.

TT157.D64 2007   745.5   C2006-906101-7

ONTARIO ARTS COUNCIL
CONSEIL DES ARTS DE L'ONTARIO

THE CANADA COUNCIL | LE CONSEIL DES ARTS
FOR THE ARTS | DU CANADA
SINCE 1957 | DEPUIS 1957

The publisher gratefully acknowledges the support of the Canada Council for the Arts and the Ontario Arts Council for its publishing program. We acknowledge the support of the Government of Ontario through the Ontario Media Development Corporation's Ontario Book Initiative.

We acknowledge the financial support of the Government of Canada through the Book Publishing Industry Development Program (BPIDP) for our publishing activities.

Key Porter Books Limited
Six Adelaide Street East, Tenth Floor
Toronto, Ontario
Canada M5C 1H6

www.keyporter.com

Design: Louise Leffler

Photography: Paul Bricknell and Maya Barkai

With thanks to Nora Rowlinson and James Montalbano for providing photoshoot locations.

Printed and bound in Singapore

07 08 09 10 11 5 4 3 2 1

Contents

Introduction

Re-creation: the act of making anew
Recreation: activity done for enjoyment

Without leaving the mall, you can buy pre-faded T-shirts with "vintage" graphics, distressed furniture with factory-applied patina, or home accessories that mimic the style of decades ago. Each gives the appearance of having a history and a soul. In reality, it's just the same mass-produced stuff that everyone else is buying.

Making something for yourself is not only enjoyable in its own right, but gives you the satisfaction of having an item that is unique. Reusing found or salvaged items conserves materials, is cost-effective, and imbues your finished product with a story much more worth retelling than "I bought it at Crate and Barrel."

The fifty projects covered in the following pages are the material equivalent of a musical remix. They take the found and the cast-off, add to them, and throw the sum into a new context for your enjoyment. Reused and re-purposed materials are the heart of the book, and our goal is to adapt materials in a simple way—to make things that function well, are pleasing to the eye, well-crafted, and pleasurable to have around.

In Getting Started (pages 10–23), you'll find background info on design plus ideas for coming up with your own projects and sourcing materials. The rest of the book is dedicated to ready-to-make projects, which include tools, techniques, and everything you need to know to get re-creative in your own home. In three categories: Furniture, Accessories, and Fabric, there's something for every object. From making a functional bedside table out of cardboard (page 65) to a lampshade from your train tickets (page 52), this book is an inspiration for turning common cast-offs into cool designs.

Getting Started

Creating a new project is a process of balancing a series of competing and interrelated decisions and requirements. To make things more challenging, when you start, you never have all the information you need to solve the problem at hand. Sometimes you'll begin with a material and figure out something to do with it, other times you'll have a need and have to come up with something to fulfill it.

Sound daunting? It's not really. By the time you're done, you'll know what it is that you want to make. You'll have an idea of what you want it to look like and what size it should be. You'll have decided what the thing will be made from and how it will be assembled. You'll figure these things out based on experience, dumb luck, and trial and error. (Okay, mostly trial and error.)

Basically, the design process takes a little bit of research, and then some experimenting and playing around until you get a result that seems right. This is not so bad. (It's quite fun actually.)

It's clear that you have some interest in projects that are appealing due to their simplicity rather than their heavily applied decoration, otherwise you'd have bought "40 Projects for Your Victorian Drawing Room," or something like that. The desire for simple, quality craftsmanship is far from an original concept, so let's first take a quick look at what has driven people in the past to create designs in this vein. A knowledge of what others have done helps channel your ideas as you work through a design. We'll then dive into some ways that materials can be reused by your average Jane and Joe and get into specifics about what to look for and where to find it.

The re-creative design process takes a little bit of research and then some experimenting and playing around until you get a result that seems right.

An Inspiration to Careful Craftsmanship

Simple, utilitarian items were the norm for most people throughout history. They were generally a means to an end and nothing more. Built to do the job, but not for appearance. Higher levels of craftsmanship were reserved for items that served a decorative need as well as a functional one. A group called the Shakers mixed this up a bit.

The desire for simple, quality craftsmanship is far from an original concept. A knowledge of what others have done helps channel your ideas as you work through a design.

The Shakers (or "The Society of United Believers" as they were officially known) were a religious group that flourished in the northeastern United States in the mid-1800s. People in this sect sought to live simply and communally, separate from the world at large, as an expression of their faith. Church doctrine prescribed celibacy, plainness in dress, speech and behavior, simplicity, thrift, and orderliness. Similarly, worldly fanciness, ornament, and superfluous possessions were forbidden.

As the sect developed, Shaker settlements farmed their own land and started producing a variety of goods, first for their own use and later for sale to generate income. The way they made their products reflected the simplicity with which they conducted their lives.

Their approach to work was of key importance to the quality of the items they made. Work was considered a noble act and was to be undertaken efficiently, skillfully, and to the best of one's ability, both for the benefit of the group and as a personal act of devotion. Craftsmanship was seen not just as desirable in itself, but as a testament of the maker's faith.

Above The Eames rocker, said to be the most significant furniture design of the twentieth century.

The resulting form of Shaker products was based on the item's function, the need for durability, and the materials used. Just as an individual in the sect focused his or her existence on worship, the products he or she made were simply and solely devoted to the purposes they served. The minimum amount of material was used to make an item sturdy and sound. Connections and detailing took into account any peculiar qualities of the materials used, for example, seasonal expansion and contraction of wood.

So here we have a model for thoughtfully creating products using humble materials, built with careful craftsmanship, to create something functional and meaningful.

Modern Design

The clean and simple lines of modern design were borne out of a reaction against unnecessary ornament and with a concern for function and efficiency in fabrication. While faith was the driving force in the Shakers' culture, early in the twentieth century new industries, a rapidly changing society, and hope for the future spurred communities of artists, designers, and architects into action.

In the first half of the century, the market's desire for profit and the shortages and urgencies of the two World Wars created a demand for strong and efficient products that spurred waves of innovation in materials and fabrication processes. Science was making it possible for products and devices that were merely fantasy a generation before to become reality.

However, many of the items that were being manufactured still mimicked the products that for centuries had been hand-produced.

Forcing new materials and methods to create something that looked "old" seemed counterintuitive to some people. Instead, they started to explore what could be achieved with the newly available materials and methods to take greater advantage of their strengths.

What they came up with were products that served their functions, but were more true to how they were made and, just like Shaker products, were minimal, finely crafted, and appealing.

The lesson here is experimentation. You can maintain values and goals for a project, while expressing it in a new or different way, based on the resources available to you (including materials, skills, and money).

We've looked at two different contexts for creation here and found some commonalities between them. Your projects may not end up looking Shaker-style or "Classic Modern," for that matter, but the values embodied in both schools of thought and the ways they were put into action are worth keeping in mind and using as inspiration.

Above This is a combination of a bent-plywood seat that was bought without legs from IKEA's "scratch and dent" department, and the rocker base from an Eames chair found *sans* seat in the Classifieds a few days later. It cost $75 altogether, but that's inexpensive compared to the alternatives available.

Junk and How to Use It

All around the world people have reused and reworked old things into new to meet the pressures of economy and necessity. Things were salvaged not because they added a certain *je ne sais quoi* to the user's home, but because the materials had a quality that could be incorporated into something else, and a value that was too good to be discarded.

Many of us may have been lucky enough not to have to live that way, but making the most of what we have and minimizing the amount that is discarded is a good way to protect our environment and our wallets.

This is one of the main differences between this book and other project books. For the most part, you won't need to run to the store to buy the materials listed. Some you'll need to acquire and accumulate and others you'll have to go hunting for. Trash is just about the only resource we're not depleting.

There are three ways to source supplies: things come to you, you stumble across something too cool to pass up, or you hunt it down.

Sourcing Recycled Materials

Before you can start to gather your materials, it usually helps to have at least a rough idea of what you'll need, although often it makes sense to acquire some things before you even have a project in mind. There are basically three ways to go about sourcing your supplies: things come to you, you stumble across something that is just too cool to pass up, or you hunt it down.

THINGS COME TO YOU

These are the sorts of things you accumulate with little effort, and include containers and packaging that you might otherwise routinely throw away. Set up a place to store them until you reach the critical mass of items needed for your project.

TOO COOL TO PASS UP

Sometimes an item catches your eye that you're sure you can do something interesting with, although what that is precisely doesn't quite spring to mind. It's a good idea to go with the hunch and pick it up. Just don't get too carried away with this or your house will end up looking like the set of *Sanford and Son*.

Because you never know what you'll come upon, it's helpful to carry a pocketknife or multi-tool with built-in screwdriver bits and pliers to enable you to strip parts off things you see set out for the trash. Sure, your pockets might be heavier, but you're being all re-creative now and it's worth it.

HUNT IT DOWN

Garage sales and flea markets are a source of unique finds, and they are also good places to find tools. Online classifieds are also a source of odd found objects. Photos often accompany the ads, so it's like wandering through a flea market from the comfort of your own desk.

Sometimes more detective work is needed. Waste generated by local businesses is a great resource. For our purposes, businesses fall into two categories. First, there are those that consistently discard the same manufactured, post-consumer items (such as carpet stores, which get rid of cardboard tubes, or a pizza place that regularly discards empty sauce jars).

The Yellow Pages are your best friend since they give an idea of where to start looking. For instance, approach appliance stores for big sheets of heavy cardboard (refrigerator boxes). Contacting a business by phone first saves you having to run around town and you may be able to talk them into holding onto some items for you or find out when things may become available.

Then there are those businesses that generate scraps and off-cuts during their fabrication process. These are especially useful if you don't need a large amount or can be flexible about size and color, etc. For example, lumberyards often have scrap bins containing pieces with defects or that are too short to store in the racks. Fabrication shops and material suppliers that work with plastics, stone, sheet metal, and upholstery also often have scrap bins.

Remember, when you're approaching a business, you're asking them to do you a favor and you should try to inconvenience them as little as possible. You need to have a good idea of what and how much of the item you'll need. Also, you may not be able to get exactly what you want, so you need to have an understanding of your project to be able to make some decisions on the fly and determine whether you can make do with the materials that are offered.

More Tips for Getting Started

✓ Plan ahead and consider if you need any tools to disassemble a scrounged item or cut it to size. Have an idea of how you'll get it home and take whatever is necessary to do so: a heavy bag, tape, rope, vehicle, your brother-in-law? Once you've got what you came for, make sure that anything you choose not to take is left neatly. Aside from just being nice, this makes it more likely that you'd be welcomed back in the future. This goes for things you pick apart on the curb, too. You don't want to make more work for the trash collectors or leave a mess someone else is going to have to clean up.

✓ When in doubt, make sure an item is free before carting it off. It sounds obvious, but sometimes a rush of creative juices to the brain can fog your commonsense.

✗ Until they've reached the end of their useful lives, avoid using things such as beer kegs, water jugs, and milk crates, which are meant to be returned and reused for their intended purpose. If you take one out of circulation, another one has to be made to take its place.

✗ Don't butcher something that has value as an antique or an historical artifact. For instance, if you're going to melt a vinyl record to make a bowl out of it, don't use a rare Charlie Parker import. Find something truly awful to sacrifice. (In fact, the world may even be a better place with one less Air Supply album in it.)

✓ If you're designing a project, try to build it so that when its life is over, it too can be reused or recycled.

✓ If using new materials, try to use those that contain recycled content and/or are recyclable. Use lumber that has been harvested from sustainable sources.

Consider your recycling ethics. Don't take a milk crate out of circulation until it's at the end of its natural life. If designing a project, try to build it so that it too can be reused or recycled.

Some Materials to Steer Clear Of

Generally it's a matter of commonsense, but sometimes it is worth being wary. Avoid containers that have held chemicals or liquids used in industry, which could pose a health hazard around the house. They are not something you want to introduce into your living space. Leftover cleaners, paints, and solvents have special disposal requirements and should not be mixed in with regular trash, but it pays to be careful. Similarly, be sure of the history of any materials that will be used around food or children.

Another caution is on electronic waste. Computers and electronics are chock-full of unpleasant heavy metals that have been associated with health risks. A computer monitor contains lead, along with a dash of mercury, cadmium, and barium. Chips and processors contain other chemicals. Capacitors may hold a residual charge long after the machine was last powered down and this means it is possible to get zapped. It's advisable to use only the cases, chassis, and miscellaneous nuts and bolts you can strip from CPUs, unless you're an electronics whiz.

If you are going to scrounge something from the trash, look things over before moving or messing with it. It's in the trash for a reason and may have sharp or broken parts.

And don't climb into dumpsters. Seriously.

Designing with Recycled Items

Ideally, you want your finished project to have the appearance and level of finish that will rival (dare we say, surpass) a store-bought item. With a limited range of recycled materials at your disposal, you may be at a disadvantage, but there are a few strategies to use that will add a quality of finish and interest to disguise this fact.

CREATE INTEREST BY USING UNORTHODOX MATERIALS

Examples would be using magazines or found art to make cards and envelopes; or making simple purses or knapsacks out of vinyl billboard material. The eye is attracted to these familiar items by the materials from which they are made. (See License Plate Box, page 26, for an example.)

USE AN OBJECT REPETITIVELY

The ordered presentation of one type of object over and over again makes an impact. Take advantage of order and regularity by using multiples of an object in a composition. Items that you purchase and discard daily are prime candidates for this purpose (see Metrocard Lampshade, page 52).

"CELEBRATE" A FOUND OBJECT

Present an item so that it is the focus of attention; this is most effective if it contrasts with its surroundings. A beat-up farm table in the corner of a barn is just that, but put it in a stark white New York City loft, and you perceive it entirely differently. A shell or tiny piece of driftwood goes unnoticed on a beach, but string it on a necklace, and it is displayed and appreciated. The presentation depends on the piece being incongruous with its surroundings and the effect can be diminished if the item is overshadowed. Any additions should be spare and minimal (see Scrap Stone Candleholder, page 32).

Of course, it goes without saying that it's a bad idea to scrounge and pilfer natural resources from the great outdoors. This is not what we mean by "reuse." Gather objects that have been discarded and then you are genuinely (and ethically) turning trash into treasure.

ALLOW THE OBJECTS TO BLEND SEAMLESSLY INTO A
NEW COMPOSITION

My favorite projects in this book are those with an interesting function that just "happen" to be made from reclaimed materials. It's as if they have a past life that only close inspection can reveal, and the fact that the project's parts are recycled takes a backseat to the new design (see Computer Case Table, page 47, for example).

USE UNUSUAL ACCESSORIES

Browse around the hardware store for interesting fasteners, handles, latches, and light bulbs. Screws that use a square drive or have recesses for an Allen wrench offer more of a finished look, as do oval head screws with trim washers. Position exposed fasteners evenly and consistently.

MIX CHEAP AND HIGH DESIGN

Humble materials have an appeal in their own right. Cardboard tubes, for example, take on a velvety texture when lightly sanded. But everything you use doesn't have to be dirt-cheap. The same design approaches can be applied to pricier components with great results. See the example of the IKEA-meets-Eames rocker on page 13.

Getting Organized

If you find yourself doing a lot of DIY projects, it's nice to have a selection of hardware on hand so you don't need to run to the store every time you need that odd screw. You can add to your stockpile by disassembling things that you're throwing away or recycling. Knobs, screws, handles, washers, gaskets, and so on are all worth scavenging if they are clean and in good shape.

If you know what you need but don't have it, you have to go looking. The first place to look is around your own home. Need a little dowel? How about a bamboo kabob stick from the kitchen? Need a bunch of small clamps? Go to the laundry room for a handful of clothes pins, or raid your desk for binder clips and rubber bands. Take an objective look at what you already have on hand and try to put it to use. Pretend you're MacGyver.

Sorting and Storage

Keep in mind that to be able to use this stuff, you need to be able to find it. It's no fun to have to dump out an entire coffee can of odds and ends to search for one little screw. Keeping things organized is a very good idea.

Look around your home for any equipment you need before rushing out to the hardware store. For example, you could use clothes pins or rubber bands as small clamps.

One way to do this is to buy a set of parts drawers. These are usually small racks filled with an array of little removable plastic drawers. This lets you sort things by type and size; say, little wood screws in this one, washers in that one, big screws in another one, and so on. You can then quickly hone in on the item you want, saving you the tedium of pawing through a big pile of things you don't need.

A homegrown alternative is to screw the lids of small jars (baby food or jelly jars work well) to the underside of a shelf. Simply fill the jars with hardware, buttons, bobbins, or whatever, and twist them into the lids so they hang in place below the shelf. While not as space-efficient as the drawers, this system is free and has been time-tested for decades in garages and basements.

Protect Yourself While Working

Odds are good that your raw materials will need some degree of preparation before they can be used in your project. This may include cutting them to size, repair, or at least a bit of cleaning. What is required will vary widely and depend on the material, its condition, and its ultimate use. However, all of these processes involve a degree of risk. Cutting, sanding, and grinding generate particles and dust. Cleaning and paint-stripping can involve harsh chemicals.

First off, you need to know how to use your tools safely and correctly. Where nifty tool techniques are needed in the projects in this book, we've included instructions, so follow these closely. Second, just as you accumulate a collection of tools to use to make your projects, you should also invest in appropriate protective gear. Use proper eye, respiratory, and hearing protection, and wear gloves, especially when using cleaners and solvents. Always follow the instructions on the product. Dust masks or respirators should be used when sanding or filing. There are different types for different uses. For example, the mask you use to protect yourself from dust won't protect you from paint fumes.

Household paints made before 1980 generally contain an amount of lead that is released as dust when sanded or scraped and inhaled into your body. You really want to avoid this. If you need to remove paint from items that date before this point, it is best done using a chemical stripper, of which there are several types on the market. In general, anything with cracked or peeling lead paint should not be allowed anywhere near children.

Dive In

Use the projects that follow to inspire you. No doubt you'll come up with your own bigger and better ideas as you look around your home and neighborhood for the cast-offs that can be transformed into stylish creations. Check out the Resources on page 142 for more help tracking down materials. Be safe. Be creative. Be resourceful. And have fun!

Time and Skill-Level Key

Each of the projects that follow is rated in terms of completion time needed and skill level.

Quick project, 1 hour max.

Medium-length project, allow a Sunday afternoon.

More ambitious project for which drying times and other waiting periods are necessary. This might take a weekend or so.

Skill level 1: Easy job for inexperienced re-creators.

Skill level 2: Requires some hardware and learning some handyman skills.

Skill level 3: Work up to these projects. You'll need to know how to keep your fingers away from the power saw (for example).

The Projects

License Plate Box

Materials

- 1 license plate
- 26-gauge galvanized steel sheet, 12" x 12"
- Scrap ½" thick plywood
- Wood finish (such as tung oil, paint, or clear polyurethane; optional)
- ¾" nails
- ½" pivot screws
- 4 washers to fit screws
- 4 stick-on rubber feet

see over for tools . . .

Make this simple "stuff" box, ideal as a pencil tin, by using an old license plate as its lid. The same processes can be applied to larger boxes, though an alternative material would have to be used for the lid. You could try using an old metal sign, for instance.

1. First, bend the very ends of the license plate down to form a "U" shape. Where the bend occurs will depend on the arrangement of letters on your particular plate, but the "legs" of the "U" need to be at least 1" long. Use the combination square to draw lines across the plate where the bends are located.

2. Clamp one end of the plate between two pieces of scrap wood, aligning the bend line with the edge of the wood. Then, pressing close to the bend line, fold the exposed portion of the plate over. Do the same for the other end of the plate.

3. Drill a ⅛" hole for the pivot screws in each of the legs at ½" from the bend line and ½" from the back edge of the leg.

4. Use tin snips to trim the steel sheet to a width of about ⅛" shorter than the distance between the bends in the license plate.

5. Mark a bend line 3¼" from each end of the steel. Following the same bending process as in step 2, make a 90-degree bend at each line to form the front, back, and base of the box.

6. Cut two pieces of plywood measuring 5½" x 3¼" to form the sides of the box.

7. The folds in the steel will be slightly rounded, so file the bottom corners of the wood pieces to match. Sand the pieces and apply

Tools

- Combination square
- Pencil
- 2 bar clamps
- 2 pieces scrap hardwood or metal angle at least 8" long
- Electric drill with 1/8" and 1/16" bits
- Tin snips
- Handsaw
- File or sandpaper
- Hammer
- Punch
- Screwdriver

a finish to them, using tung oil, paint, or clear polyurethane, if you wish.

8. On the steel sheet front and back of the box, mark locations at each corner for the nails that will hold the sides in place. Dimple the locations with the hammer and punch, then pre-drill the nail hole with the 1/16" bit.

9. Put the wood sides in place and drive the nails through the holes into the steel sheet and then into the wood.

10. Slip the cover into place on top of the box. The next step is to determine the location for the pivot screws. They need to be placed in a way that keeps the lid from binding when it is flipped up. Experiment a bit to find the right spot, then drill a 1/16" hole into the ends of the box.

11. Screw the pivot screws into the wood sides with a washer between the wood and the license plate and another between the plate and the head of the screw.

12. Apply four rubber stick-on feet to the bottom of the box.

Necktie Cushion

Time: 🕐   **Skill:** ٦٦

Materials

- At least 12 men's ties
- 20" pillow form (or desired size)
- Lightweight iron-on interfacing
- Thread
- Embellishments, e.g. piping, cording, trim, buttons, fancy threads (optional)
- ¾ yd fabric for back of pillow
- 2¼ yd edging trim (optional)
- Pins
- Zipper (length determined by the size of cushion; optional)

see over for tools . . .

So you are getting rid of your scrappy old ties or, the man in your life is upgrading. To someone who sews, that means free fabric. But what can you do with a bunch of old ties? Here is a quick home furnishing project, which for intermediate or advanced sewers offers opportunities for quilting and embellishing. For those with intermediate sewing skills, the instructions on how to cut them up and make them into a throw pillow are easy to follow. Let your creativity take hold.

1. Wash the ties either by hand or in the washer. If you choose the washer, wash as many ties as possible at one time on the "delicates" cycle. To avoid pulling a huge knot of ties out at the end of the cycle, wash the ties within a pillowcase. Hang them separately to dry.

2. Cut the seam thread at both ends of each tie and pull it through. Discard the white stabilizer fabric. If you wish, cut off the points, and save them to use as an embellishment in this or a future project. Remove any lining material on the ties.

3. Iron the tie fabric on both sides. Because ties are cut on the bias, you will find that they stretch. To help prevent this from happening and to keep the edges from fraying, press some lightweight iron-on interfacing to the back of the fabric. You are now ready to cut the fabric into strips.

4. Decide how wide you wish to cut each strip to create your design. For the tie pillow shown on page 30, we used the rotary cutter to cut strips 2" wide along the full length of the ties. For information on how to use a rotary cutter, see Techniques (page 139).

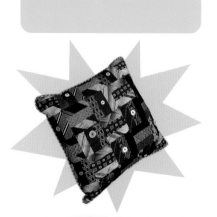

Tools

- Scissors
- Iron
- Straightedge or quilter's ruler
- Rotary cutter
- Sewing machine

5. With right sides together, take a ¼" seam to sew the strips together and form blocks of fabric to your desired pattern. If the blocks don't quite fit the pillow form, consider adding a border to make up any difference. The blocks used in the pictured pillow are made up of three 2" strips stitched together and then trimmed to make 4½" squares.

6. The next step is to be creative. Quilt the top, use special stitching with fancy thread, cording, hand embroidery, machine embroidery, add buttons (regular or specialty)—whatever strikes your fancy.

7. Now complete the pillow cover. First cut the back fabric to the size of the pillow form, plus 1" extra on all sides. Pin the front to the back, right sides together.

8. To add piping around the edges, sandwich the piping between the decorated front cover and the back fabric facing inwards, and with fabrics right side together. Stitch a ¼" seam on three sides, using the zipper foot on the sewing machine. Leave the fourth side open.

9. If you plan to put in a zipper, use the zipper foot to stitch one side of the zipper along one open edge of the pillow cover. Turn the cover right-side out and then stitch the other side of the zipper to the remaining edge to complete. Insert the pillow form and zip up the open edge. If you do not wish to insert a zipper, simply slip-stitch the open side to complete.

Variation: Used Clothing Quilt

If you want to make a larger item, for example a quilt, you will need larger pieces of material such as all those old clothes that you no longer wear. Follow exactly the same steps as for the cushion but on a much larger scale.

Scrap Stone Candleholder

Materials

- Scrap limestone from a construction site
- Stick-on felt (optional)
- Candles

Tools

- Pencil
- Straightedge
- Electric drill with ¾" masonry bit
- Brush

A stout and unusual candleholder can be made from scrap building stone. Indiana limestone, as used in this example, is a common stone widely used for the exterior components of masonry building. It is relatively soft and easy to mill, making it possible to work with an electric drill using a masonry bit. Harder stones such as granite require more specialized equipment to shape them.

Look in Yellow Pages for building stone fabricators in your area. They generally have bins of scrap material and may be willing to give you a few pieces. If there is no usable stone available to you, you could achieve a similar look using a solid cinder block.

1. Based on the shape of the scrap stone, decide how many candles you want to use and where you want them to go. Use the pencil and straightedge to mark where you need to drill holes. Ensure that the stone will not tip over when the candles are installed.

2. Drill holes in the stone approximately 1" deep. In limestone or cinder block, it will be pretty easy work.

3. Blow the dust out of the holes, scrub the stone with a brush and water, and let it dry thoroughly.

4. Apply the adhesive felt to the bottom of the stone to avoid damaging any furniture it's set on.

5. Make sure the candles fit snugly in the base and aren't prone to tipping. If the hole is too small for the candle, you can use a knife to shave the base of the candle to the correct size. If the hole is too big, wrap the base with electrical tape until it fits the hole well. Of course, never leave candles burning unattended.

Floppy Disk Photo Holder

Time: 🕐 **Skill:** ↖

Materials

- Floppy disks
- Block of wood

Tools

- Glue

This is a simple and effective way to make use of all those obsolete floppy disks, which are ending up in landfills in very large numbers since we now use other methods of storage like CDs, or portable hard drives.

1. Remove the aluminum rectangle piece from the floppy carefully. For each photo holder you will need one of these aluminum rectangles.

2. For the base, you will need a block of wood. You could use a piece from a child's building block set, but old Lego or plastic blocks can also make good bases, or you can cut a piece of wood to fit. Make sure it is sufficiently weighty.

3. Glue the aluminum rectangle to one end of the wooden block, leaving the gap at the top to insert the photograph.

4. Once the glue is dry, your photograph holder is ready to use.

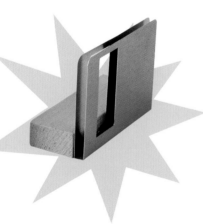

Tip You can also use these as place settings at dinner parties, placing a name card in the holder for each of your guests.

Tripod Lamp

Time: 🕐	Skill: ⌃⌃

Materials

- Aluminum tube ⅛" thick, 1½" square, 3" long
- Lamp socket with built-in switch
- Bulb
- Shade harp (support)
- 1" threaded lamp rod
- Nut or sleeve to fit lamp rod
- Plug
- Nut to fit tripod mounting screw
- Tripod
- Lamp shade

Tools

- Hacksaw
- File(s)
- Sandpaper
- Electric drill with bits
- Wire cutter/stripper
- Straight blade screwdriver

With just one piece of tube, you can turn a garage sale tripod into a surprisingly versatile lamp. By extending the legs, it can be converted from a table lamp to a floor lamp. Remove the shade and screw in a spotlight that can be pivoted by the tripod head.

And by removing one nut on the fixture you can use the tripod to hold a camera!

1. Cut the aluminum tube to size with the hacksaw and smooth the cut edges using a file and sandpaper.

2. 1" from the end of one face of the tube, drill a hole large enough for the mounting screw to pass through.

3. Drill a ½" hole in the opposite face of the tube and 1" from the other end.

4. File any burrs from the holes.

To wire the lamp socket:

5. Press the side of the socket where it says "press" and pull the socket apart, to make two halves. This will expose the internal base of the socket (see Fig. 1 and 2).

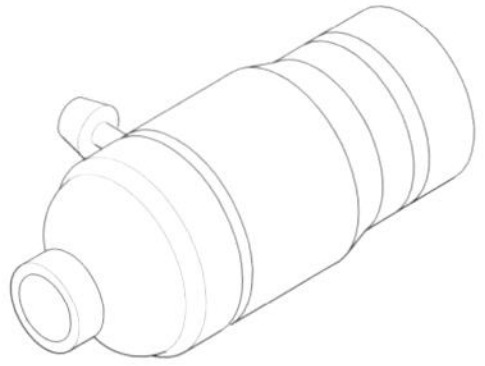

Fig. 1

6. Lamp cord consists of two parallel, insulated wires that are fused together. Slip the lamp base over the end of the cord; separate the two wires and then tie them together in a knot 2" from their ends. The knot

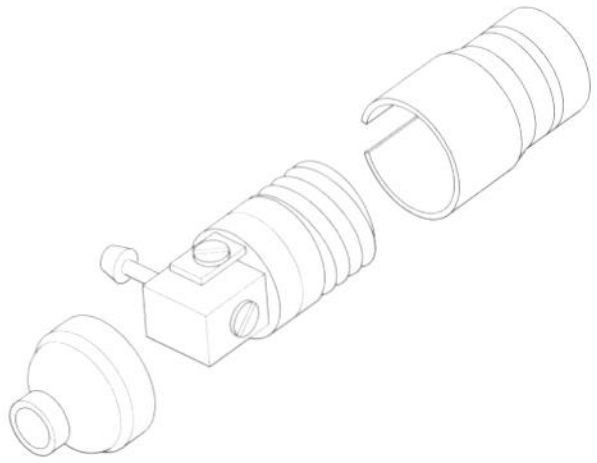

Fig. 2

should be big enough to prevent the cord from being pulled back through the base (see Fig. 3).

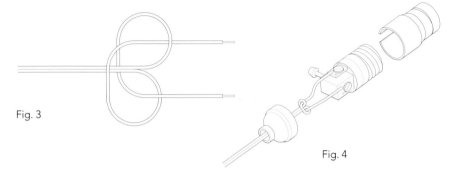

Fig. 3

Fig. 4

7. Cut the wires 1¼" beyond the knot and strip off from the end ½" of insulation. Twist the insulation as you slide it off to bind the internal strands of wire together.

8. Loosen the two screws on the sides of the socket. Bend one of the uninsulated wire ends into a hook shape and wrap it clockwise around the posts of one of the screws. It should wrap tight as you tighten up the screw. Do the same for the other wire and screw (see Fig. 4).

9. Slide the upper half of the socket down over the base and press the two together until you hear them click and lock in place. Make sure that no wires are pinched inside and that they aren't too crowded in the base. (See Fig. 5.)

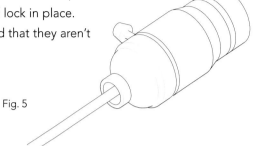

Fig. 5

10. Thread the lamp rod into the base of the lamp socket and tighten the screw in the base to clamp the rod in place.

11. Run the end of the lamp cord through the shade harp (support) and then through the $\frac{1}{2}$" hole in the tube. Slide the lamp rod through the hole in the base of the harp and then through the $\frac{1}{2}$" hole in the tube. Slide the lamp rod nut over the cord, thread it onto the lamp rod, and draw it down tight.

12. Attach the plug to the end of the cord (follow the manufacturer's instructions).

13. Slip the smaller hole in the tube over the tripod mounting screw, and use the remaining nut to hold it in place.

14. Install the bulb and the shade and you're ready to go.

Plastic Strap Bench

Materials

- Poplar or other hardwood for:

  2 side rails: 1¼" x 1½" x 4½ ft

  2 end rails: 1¼" x 3½" x 12"
- ½" Phillips panhead screws
- Wood finish (such as tung oil or clear polyurethane; optional)
- Eight 2" #10 flathead wood screws
- 4 legs (scrounged, bought, or homemade), with screws
- ⅝" diameter dowel, 13" long
- Plastic strapping

  see over for tools . . .

Time: 🕐   **Skill:** ٦٦٦

The heavy plastic strapping used for this bench seat was originally used to bind together large stacks of lumber during shipping. As you would imagine, it's pretty strong stuff. When the lumber arrives at its destination, the straps are cut and discarded. Take a quick walk through the aisles of a home center and you will find plenty of pieces either lying on the floor or about the racks. After a few visits, you can accumulate enough material to web a decent-sized bench.

The design shown in the picture opposite is a basic idea, but there are many ways to customize your own style. For example, shorten to make a stool, or use a different style of leg. The legs used here were scrounged from a pair of discarded chairs.

To build the frame:

1. Cut the dowel and the side and end rails to size.

2. At the midpoint of one of the 1½" faces of each side rail, drill a ½" deep hole. The diameter of the hole should match the diameter of the dowel. If your bench will be 2 feet or less in length, you can skip this step and eliminate the dowel.

3. Insert one end of the dowel in each of the holes and clamp the end rails between the side rails. Align the tops of the end pieces with the tops of the side pieces and let the side rails run 2" past the end rails (see Fig. 1).

4. Pre-drill, countersink, and install two screws, spaced 2" apart, through the side rails into each end of the end rails.

Fig. 1

Tools

- Handsaw
- Electric drill with drill bits
- Screwdriver bit
- Two 18" bar clamps
- Fine file or sandpaper
- T-square or framing square (a sheet of poster board will work in a pinch)
- Tape measure
- Pencil
- Fine-tip marker pen
- Tin snips
- Pliers

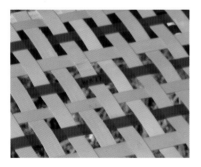

5. Once the frame has been screwed together, sand the frame and apply a finish, if you like.

To prepare the straps:

6. Cut the straps into 21" lengths using the tin snips, and try to avoid any stains, labeling, or obvious damage. The number of straps required will depend on the length of the bench, but assume 12 straps for every foot of the bench's length, then cut a few extra. Also cut nine pieces that are each the length of the bench plus 9".

7. Place the frame on the floor or a table, with the underside facing up. Lay a strap across the middle of the bench and on the bottom of one of the side rails; mark with a pencil where the sides of the strap reach. From each mark, make additional marks at 1" intervals down the rail. Then lay the square across the frame and transfer these marks across onto the other rail. (At the ends you may need to tweak the interval a bit to get the straps to cover the heads of the screws that hold the frame together.) These marks will help you keep the straps straight and evenly spaced across the frame. Do the same thing on the end rails.

To install the straps:

8. Grip the end of a strap in the pliers 1½" from the end and fold the strap at 90 degrees, at a point right beside the pliers' jaws. Release the strap, and by hand, bend the fold further to 180 degrees, then squeeze the fold line with the pliers to crease the plastic.

9. Unfold the strap back to 90 degrees and align the short leg of the fold with the center strap marks on the underside of the frame. Use the drill with a screwdriver bit to drive one of the panhead screws through the strap into the frame (see Fig. 2).

10. Hold the strap up to the edge of the frame, mark where the next fold is to occur, pull the strap away, pinch it, fold it, and crimp it. Follow the same procedure until you've wrapped the strap around to the other side. Then screw the other end in place. Do this for all of the short straps. Before marking each fold, pull the strap tight to locate the mark correctly. The goal is to have the straps as taut as possible once both ends are screwed down. If a strap is too saggy, try to reinstall it or discard it and make a new one (see Fig. 3).

11. The process for attaching the long straps is similar: Just weave them between the short strips as you work from one end to the other.

12. Once all the straps are installed, use the tin snips to trim off any excess strapping on the underside of the frame. File any sharp corners on the cut ends of the straps.

13. Attach the legs to the underside of the end rails.

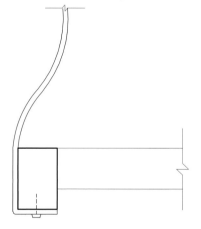

Fig. 2

Fig. 3

Pizza Pan Table

Time: 🕐 **Skill:** ✓✓

Materials

- 16" pizza pan
- Two 4 ft aluminum strips, ¾" x ⅛"
- 8 pop rivets
- One ½" machine screw and nut to fit

Tools

- Pencil
- Electric drill with ⅛" drill bit
- 2" wide masking tape
- 4" steel post
- Vise (or 1 bar clamp and 2 blocks of hardwood)
- Large piece of paper
- Combination square
- Compass
- Tape measure
- Scissors
- Pop riveter

Here's an ideal little table to hold your beer and chips while you're outside in the yard or inside, sitting on the living-room floor watching the game. It's all aluminum, so it's lightweight, weather-proof, and entirely recyclable. The aluminum strips are widely available in 4 ft lengths, so you can make the whole thing without having to do any cutting.

1. Draw reference lines across each of the aluminum strips as shown in Fig. 1. These will help ensure that the bends are made in the same spot on each of the table legs.

2. In the middle of the center mark on each strip, drill a ⅛" hole. Then drill holes ½" and 1¼" from each end of each strip.

3. On a piece of masking tape, draw three parallel lines, 1¼" apart. Then stick the tape onto the post. The post will be used as a form to bend the aluminum strips around. A 4" steel post (like you find in many home cellars) is ideal, but a rigid tube of some sort 3–4" in diameter will do the job.

4. Align mark A on one of the strips with the middle line on the tape. Bend the strip around the post until the B marks meet the outer marks on the tape. Do the same on the other end of the strip.

5. Align the center mark on the strip with the center mark on the tape and make the slight center bend.

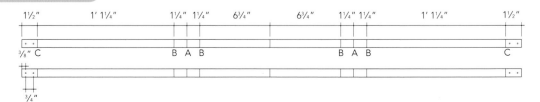

1½"	1' 1¼"	1¼" 1¼"	6¾"	6¾"	1¼" 1¼"	1' 1¼"	1½"

⅜" C   B A B   B A B   C

Fig. 1

¾"

Pizza Pan Table

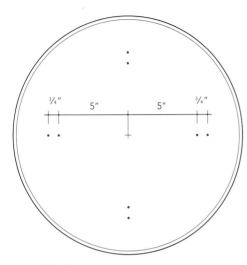

Fig. 2

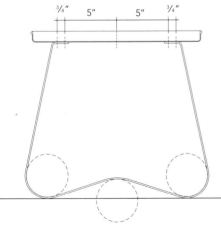

Fig. 3

6. Clamp one end of the strip in the vise, aligning line C with the edge of the jaws, and make a sharp bend. Do the same on the other end of the strip. If no vise is available, clamp the bar between two blocks of hardwood instead.

7. Repeat steps 4–6 with the other strip. When the pieces are roughly formed, compare them to one another and fine-tune them until they match. Bend the curves tighter or open them up until they closely align with each other.

8. Drill holes in the pizza pan 5″ and 5¾″ from the center, at 12, 3, 6, and 9 o'clock. To lay out the hole locations, cut a piece of paper into a circle that fits just inside the rim of the pan. Fold the circle into quarters, cut two little notches in the edge, 5″ and 5¾″ from the center, then unfold the paper. Lay it in the pan and use the resulting openings in the paper to mark the hole locations on the pan (see Fig. 2).

9. Place one of the legs underneath the pan, align the holes in the pieces, and pop-rivet them together. Small screws can also be used, but the heads of the rivets are very flat, allowing you to set a glass right on top of them without rocking or tipping (see Fig. 3).

10. Once one leg is riveted to the pan, put the second in place and make sure the table doesn't rock. Adjust the middle bend of the second leg to keep the table from rocking, then rivet it to the pan as well.

11. Last, insert the screw through the holes where the legs overlap and tighten the nut.

Computer Case Table

Time: 🕐   Skill: ⚒⚒

Materials

- 2 CPU covers, one horizontal, one vertical
- 2 pieces wood, plywood, or MDF, each 8" x 18"
- Handful 6" x ¾" panhead screws
- Spray paint
- 4 rubber feet

Tools

- Tape measure
- Straightedge
- Pencil
- Handsaw or circular saw
- Electric drill with ⅛" drill bit
- Screwdriver
- File
- Medium to fine sandpaper
- Silicone sealant and caulk gun

In urban areas, it's common to see old computer cases (CPUs) set out with the trash. Fortunately, one of the simplest parts of a computer to reuse also happens to be one of the easiest to swipe off the curb: the big, dumb, U-shaped piece of metal that covers the chassis. They come in different sizes and depths and are shaped to cover either vertically or horizontally configured CPUs. Often these simply slide off from the rest of the computer or at most are held on with a few screws. Either way, you can easily grab yourself the makings of a new end table.

Alternately, if you don't want to scavenge, look in Yellow Pages for companies that recycle computers and components. They've usually got plenty of covers lying around. Net yourself a pair to make this simple little table/magazine rack.

1. Before you start, thoroughly wash the sheet metal pieces you've scrounged and leave them to dry while you cut the wood.

2. The table base is made from the vertical case and two pieces of wood that form its top and back. Cut both pieces of wood to match the case width. Cut the back piece to match the case height but cut the top piece 2" shy of the case's depth.

3. Slip the back piece into position as shown in Fig. 1. Attach the wood back by screwing into it through the existing holes in the metal at the rear of the case. Pre-drill screw holes in the wood first so that the wood doesn't split.

4. Drill two new holes in the upper edge of each side of the case and put the top piece of wood into place. Use the file to smooth off any burrs. The surface of the wood should sit flush with the

top edge of the case. Screw the wood through the new holes to attach the top.

5. To prepare the tabletop, set the horizontal case into position and drill two holes in the lip at its rear and file the holes smooth. You'll need these holes to attach the top to the base. Do not screw it in place yet.

6. Now paint the two halves of the table. A light sanding to take the sheen off the existing paint will help the new finish to adhere.

7. Once you've applied a few coats of paint, you can join the halves. First, use sandpaper to rough up the underside of the tabletop where it will rest on the base. Then, on the top of the base, squeeze out a few generous beads of silicone sealant, following the manufacturer's instructions. Center the tabletop on the base and install the last two screws. (See Fig. 2 and 3.)

8. Let the silicone cure, stick the rubber feet onto the bottom of the base, and then load the table up with your favorite magazines.

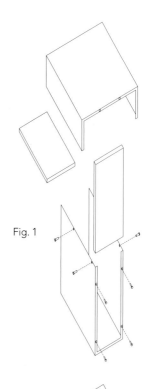

Fig. 1

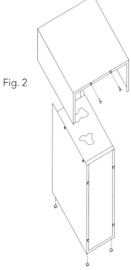

Fig. 2

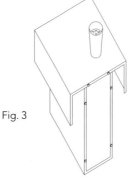

Fig. 3

Foam Frame

Materials

- Foam packaging
- Glass or plastic to fit opening in foam
- Photograph
- Pins
- Bamboo skewer

Tools

- Bread knife
- Fine-tip marker pen
- Straightedge
- Scissors
- Craft glue or wood glue
- Glass cutter (if cutting your own glass)

Computers and electronic equipment come packaged in foam nests that protect them during shipping. The piece used here was packaging for a new hard drive and made for a simple frame almost right out of the box.

1. Find two pieces of foam, one with a recess that will form the frame and a second, flat piece for the prop on the back. With luck, the piece for the frame is ready to go as is. However, if you need to trim or shape a larger block of foam to get a usable piece, use a bread knife to cut it quickly and cleanly.

2. One edge of the prop will need to sit flat on the tabletop and an adjacent edge is to be glued perpendicular to the back of the frame. The prop needs to be roughly triangular shape. The frame needs to lean back to resist tipping over, so cut the edge of the prop at an angle. Experiment to find an angle that is suitable. It's a good idea to cut it oversize at first with a fairly steep angle. Draw a cutting line on the foam using the marker and straight-edge and cut along it with the scissors. Attach the prop with the pins to try it out. If it's too steep, trim the edge back a little more.

3. Once everything is stable, trim any extra material off the prop piece. Remove the prop, apply the glue and put it back in place. Pin to hold it in place while the glue dries.

4. Cut the glass or plastic to fit into the opening in the frame. It ought to be just a little bigger than the opening, so the foam squeezes it when it is put in place over the photograph.

5. If necessary, insert a bamboo skewer into the prop to stiffen it.

Metrocard Lampshade

Time: 🕐   **Skill:** ⋌⋌

Materials

- Lots of cards
- Lots of jump rings ½"
  in diameter
- Scrap of plywood,
  approximately 8" x 12"
- Scrap cardboard
- Lampshade frame

Tools

- ¹⁄₁₆" hole punch
- Needle-nosed pliers
- Coping saw
- Strong rubber band
- Utility knife
- Tape
- Craft glue

Metrocards have taken the place of tokens in the New York City subway system and while they're reusable, it's inevitable that people accumulate expired ones. But you don't have to live in New York to make a similar lamp as the same process can be applied using old business cards, incomplete decks of playing cards, or baseball cards.

Take care to use a lampshade frame that will keep the cards well away from the light bulb. A large-size frame will also allow the cards to form a gentler curve and keep the lampshade from looking too faceted. Lampshade frames are available from craft stores, though you can reuse an old or damaged shade. The top and bottom hoops need to be the same size.

Aside from the cards and the frame, the other component of the shade is the jump rings. These are little wire rings used in jewelry making, which can be bought from craft stores.

The key to this project is to position the holes in the same place on all of the cards. The easiest and quickest way to do this accurately is to make a jig to punch the holes.

1. First, determine where the holes need to be on the cards. To hang them in the pattern shown here, you need to make holes at quarter and three-quarter points across the top and bottom of the cards. When the cards are clipped together, there should be a little space left between them. When you have a card that works well, mark it and put it aside to use as the master card.

To make the jig:

2. Use the coping saw to cut a "U" shape into the edge of the plywood so that the bottom jaw of the hole punch fits snugly into

it. You need the wood to prevent the punch from twisting or wobbling while still letting you squeeze the handles to punch holes.

3. Take the master card and close the hole punch on it so that the male half of the punch passes through the pre-punched hole. Wrap a rubber band around the handles of the punch to keep the jaws closed.

4. Take two pieces of cardboard and tack and glue them onto the wood alongside two edges of the card. Remove the rubber band and the punched card. This completes the jig.

To assemble the lampshade:

5. Place a new card against the edges of the cardboard on the jig, and punch a hole. Flip the card over and do the next corner and repeat until you have a hole in each corner of the card. Just make sure you don't let the card slip under the edges of the cardboard guides. Pop your favorite music on and punch all of your cards.

6. Once all the cards are punched, use the jump rings to clip them together. Open the rings by twisting them sideways. Don't pull them apart. When you close the rings, twist them back until you hear the ends click against each other. A pair of needle-nosed pliers will make the process easier on your fingers.

7. Attach the top ring of the shade frame to a lamp and start clipping the cards on, staggering the cards like bricks at each row. After a few rows, the pattern will begin to emerge. At the bottom of the shade, clip the cards to the bottom rim of the frame.

Novelty Clocks

Time: 🕐   **Skill:** ↖

Materials

- Item to use as the clock face
- Battery-operated clock movement

Tools

- Scrap wood
- Electric drill with selection of twist bits
- Needle-nose and regular pliers
- Wire cutters

A clock face can be made out of just about anything that you can drill a hole through—from roof slates to circuit boards, from LPs to books. All of the clocks shown here are based around a pre-assembled, self-contained movement (the mechanism that makes the clock run). These come in many degrees of complexity, accuracy, and cost, and are available with different length sleeves to accomodate clock faces of different thicknesses. If all you need is something to tell you how much time you have until Star Trek comes on, a simple AA battery-operated quartz movement will be fine. These can be purchased online and at most stores that sell craft or woodworking supplies.

Typically, the movement consists of a small plastic box which measures 2″ x 2″ and contains the moving parts and the battery. Connected to the center of the box is a threaded metal sleeve that is used to attach the movement to the face of the clock.

1. Once you've chosen your object for the clock, you need to drill a hole through its "face." The hole should be large enough to accommodate the threaded sleeve of the movement. However, if you're working with a tough material such as metal or dense plastic, start with a small drill bit and work up to the final size bit in a few steps. It will be easier to drill and will result in a cleaner hole.

2. The movement will come with the hardware required and installation instructions. Attaching the movement usually involves slipping a rubber washer over the threaded sleeve, poking the sleeve through the hole in the clock face, and threading a washer and a thin nut onto it. Then the hands are slipped on and a tiny retaining nut is screwed on. That's really all there is to it.

Novelty Clocks

Tea Tin Clock

This table clock started life as a tea tin picked up in a Chinese grocery. The fabrication is pretty straightforward and, in this case, the mouth of the tin was large enough to accommodate the movement. Make sure the hands are short enough to clear the table at 6.30.

LP or '45 Sleeve Clock

All you need to make this one is an old album sleeve, a utility knife, and some thick scrap cardboard. Two tabs were cut and folded out of the back to allow it to stand up. Some scrap cardboard was slipped into the jacket and glued into place for added rigidity.

Hubcap Clock

The hubcap clock is the simplest clock to attempt. It's really just a VW hubcap with a hole drilled in it. The movement has a slot molded into the back that allows it to hang on a wall.

Crushed Can Clock

The trick here is to squash the can in an aesthetically pleasing manner. So when you drive over it, place the side of the can against the tire tread and roll over it a few times. (If your neighbors don't already look at you strangely, this should do it.) Squash any remaining high spots with a pair of pliers.

Scale Clock

A perpetually incorrect bathroom scale was gutted to make this clock. The internal springs were removed and the original dial was used as the face. Wire cutters were used to trim the hands to just the right length. Some tape and shims were used to hold the face in position before the scale was reassembled and hung on the bathroom wall.

Bucket Baskets

Time: 🕐 **Skill:** ⌇⌇⌇

Materials

- Large sheet of paper
- Two 5-gallon plastic buckets
- Cord or heavy string
- 10 rivets

Tools

- Pencil
- Ruler or straightedge
- Scissors
- Scotch tape
- Fine-tip marker pen
- Electric drill with ⅛"
  and ⅜" drill bits
- Electric jigsaw
- Utility knife
- Fine file
- 150- and 220-grit sandpaper
- Rivet tool
- Hammer
- Spring clamps or binder
  clips

Five-gallon plastic buckets are ubiquitous. They're used to hold paint, drywall compound, and even bulk food products. For this project, you'll need two buckets to make the large basket and the leftovers can be used to make up the smaller basket.

To make the large basket:

1. Reproduce patterns A and B from page 61 and cut them out. For the cross-shaped piece, cut it out like a paper snowflake: fold the sheet in half, and in half again, and then trace one quarter of the pattern onto the folded sheet (see Fig. 1). Cut out the pattern and unfold to reveal the whole template.

2. Remove the metal handles from the buckets.

3. Wrap the cross pattern (Pattern B) around one of the buckets and tape it in place, taking care to keep the centerline perpendicular to the bottom of the bucket (see Fig. 2).

4. Mark around the pattern onto the bucket using the marker, then remove the paper pattern. (When the long ends of the pattern wrap around, they meet at an angle due to the fact that the bucket tapers. Just round off this angle a little when tracing the pattern.)

5. Use the drill with the ⅜" bit to make starter holes along the pattern line. Insert the blade of the jigsaw into a hole and carefully saw along the marker line to cut the shape out of the bucket.

6. Trace two of the trapezoid shapes (Pattern A) onto opposite sides of the second bucket. Align the wide end of the pattern with the bottom edge of the bucket rim, and mark as before. Drill a couple of starter holes, then cut out these shapes (see Fig. 3).

Bucket Baskets

Fig. 1

Fig. 2

Fig. 3

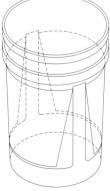

7. Use the utility knife to fine-tune the cutouts if necessary, and sand all the edges with a fine file.

8. Drill two ⅛" holes in the tabs of the hoop piece (see pattern A). Center the wide edge of one of the trapezoid pieces on the base of the tab and drill two matching holes. Then, using the hammer and rivet tool, install two rivets to hold the pieces together. The tab should be on the outside face of the basket. Do the same with the other trapezoid piece.

9. Bend the tab to bring the ears of the trapezoid pieces up to the base of the handle. Make sure they line up evenly, then drill and rivet the ears to the handle base. It's helpful to clamp the pieces together during the drilling process.

10. Drill two ⅛" holes in the handle to provide a place to tie off the cord handle wrap, then wrap the handle with cord or string.

To make the small basket:

1. Use the leftover portion of the second bucket from which you cut the trapezoid pieces. Mark a line around the bucket 2" up from the bucket's base (see Fig. 3).

2. Lay out two 1½" wide handle strips vertically up opposite sides of the bucket. Round off the corner where the handle meets the base.

3. Cut the shape out of the bucket, sand the edges and round over the ends of the handle straps.

4. Bend the straps until they overlap and clamp them together. Drill a pair of holes and install two rivets to bind the handle straps.

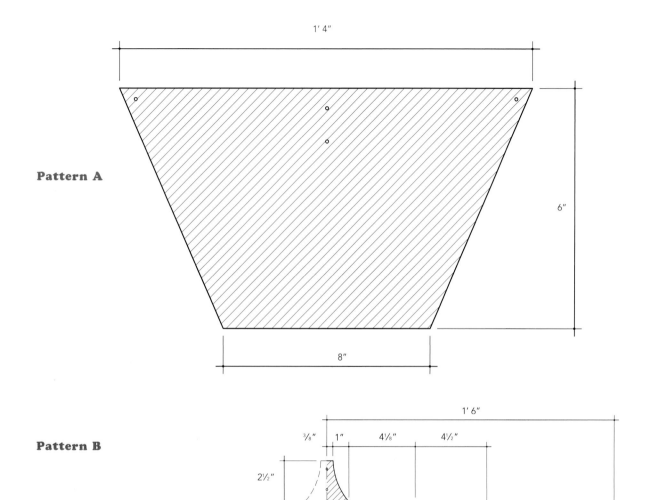

Pattern A

1' 4"

6"

8"

Pattern B

1' 6"

3/8"
1"
4 1/8"
4 1/2"

2 1/2"

3"

3/8"

CD Rack Table

Time: 🕐 **Skill:** ϟϟϟ

Materials

- 2 wooden CD racks
- 2 sides of a wooden CD rack
- 8 screws
- Primer
- Black acrylic paint
- Printers type tray
- Two wooden blocks slightly smaller than the width of the tray and ¾" to 1" thick
- Wood glue

Tools

- Hacksaw
- Electric drill
- Screwdriver
- Paintbrush

As more and more of our music collections are stored on computers or MP3 players, we all have old CD racks going to waste. Instead of throwing them away, they can be used to create a beautiful new side table that also doubles as storage for all those CDs you can't quite bear to throw away.

To make the table base:

1. Use the hacksaw to cut the two sides of the CD rack to the width you require for the table. If the rack you're using doesn't have extra pieces left over to make the "bridges," you have a couple of other options you can use to create your table bases. Either cut pieces the correct size from scrap wood, or sandwich the towers between strips of lumber or sheets of plywood attached to the sides of the towers.

2. These pieces are used to form a bridge between the two CD towers to make the table more sturdy. One should sit about 3" underneath the table top, with the other about 3" from the bottom.

3. Make a mark on the CD towers where you want to attach the bridges and drill four holes for each bridge, then attach the bridges using the screws.

4. Paint the table base with primer, then follow with two coats of black acrylic paint.

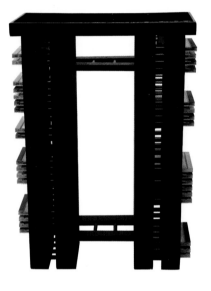

To make the table top:

5. The two wooden blocks are used to attach the table top to the CD rack base. Center the tray you are using for the table top over the table base and make a pencil mark to indicate where the blocks need to be glued to line up with the slots on the top of the two CD racks. This means the tray is removable, but will ensure that it fits over the base and does not slide or move around.

6. Glue the blocks to the bottom of the tray.

7. Prime the tray and then follow with two coats of black paint.

To decorate the table top:

8. This table is finished with a mosaic created from pages from a comic. To do something similar, follow the instructions for the decoupage tray on page 123. If a simple paint job is good enough for you, go get a snack and put your new table to use.

Tip Instead of comics or cartoons, photographs, wood, or carpet samples can be used to create a mosaic effect. An Asian look can be achieved by using a combination of red, gold, and black acrylic paints. Using origami paper and gold leaf would result in an expensive lacquer effect.

Stackable Cardboard Table

Time: 🕐   **Skill:** ↖

Materials

- Double wall corrugated cardboard
- Clear paste wax

Tools

- Utility knife
- Straightedge
- Pencil
- Wood glue
- Clothes pins or small clamps

Like the felt-covered table on page 86, these tables are made from double wall corrugated cardboard for maximum strength. Since they're entirely made out of cardboard, they are simple and cost practically nothing to make. Their shape also allows for them to be stacked on top of one another and nest together for storage.

For a more finished appearance than described, decoupage the surface with scraps of colored paper or magazine clippings (see page 123). Paint is another option, but experiment on scrap beforehand. Spray paint on cardboard rarely comes out looking good.

Alternatively, you could let your child go at it with finger paints. Play around. The table is basically free, so if you don't like the results, recycle it and make another one.

1. Reproduce patterns A and B from page 66. Using the knife and straightedge, cut the shapes from the corrugated cardboard as follows: Each table will require one piece of A and four pieces of B.

2. Score the pieces as shown by the dashed lines in the diagram. For tips on scoring cardboard cleanly, see Techniques (page 139).

3. Carefully fold the pieces along the score lines. The arms of the cross-shaped piece should swing down so their edges meet, forming the top and sides of the table.

4. Glue the legs inside the corners where the sides meet. In addition to supporting the table, the legs also serve to secure the joint between the sides. Clamp the pieces in place until the glue dries.

5. To protect the table against spills, rub on a coat of clear paste wax.

Stackable Cardboard Table

Pattern A

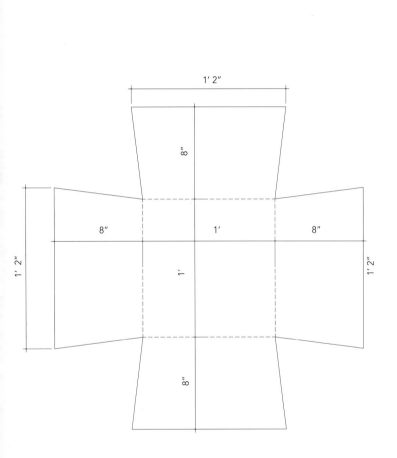

Pattern B

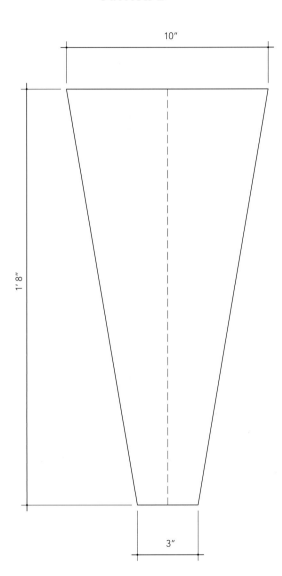

Negative Lamps

Materials

- Broken candle holder
- Sheet of perforated metal
- Lamp holder and mechanism
- Nuts and bolts
- Negatives
- Plastic folders

Time: 🕐   **Skill:** ↖

Tools

- Double-sided sellotape
- Scissors

Old or broken candle holders can have a new lease of life as lamps, recycling the electrical mechanism from any lamps that you no longer use. You can use any old negatives to create a sepia effect that looks really stunning when lit from within. However, be sure to use a small, low-wattage bulb and socket to avoid overheating.

Negative Tower

1. This lamp began life as a candleholder with one pane of glass missing. To replace a missing pane of glass, cut a piece of perforated metal to the same dimensions as the other panes and fit it to the lamp. The perforations will allow the light to come through and adds an industrial look that complements the negatives.

2. Attach the lamp mechanism to the the metal sheet using nuts and bolts.

3. Cut negatives to fit each side of the lamp. Make a random pattern for each side by using the negatives both horizontally and vertically.

4. Cut the plastic folders to the same dimensions as the panes of glass. Use double-sided sellotape to attach the negatives to the plastic, then sandwich the negatives between the plastic and the glass pane.

Negative Lamps

Hanging Negative Lamp

1. To make the second lamp, follow exactly the same procedure as for the negative tower, only this time using a hanging lantern.

2. To insert the negatives, remove the screws in the top of the lantern to remove the glass pane. Sandwich the negatives between the glass pane and the plastic folder before returning the panes to the lamp and screwing everything back into place.

Tip Colored tissue, transparent paper, skeleton leaves, or handmade paper can all be used to create interesting effects. To create an abstract pattern, use colored sellotape on paper. Parchment or greaseproof paper are good substitutes for the file covers. As always with lights, be careful not to let any flammable materials too close to a hot bulb.

Lawn Chair Wind Chime

Time: 🕐 **Skill:** ᴦᴦ

Materials

- Lawn chair
- End cap for 4", schedule-40 PVC pipe
- Spool fishing line
- Wood ball 1½" in diameter
- An item to serve as a wind catcher
- 2 fishing swivels
- 1 metal or plastic ring
- 1 plastic bead

Tools

- Coarse file
- Pliers
- Tubing cutter
- 220-grit sandpaper
- Steel wool
- Electric drill with ⅛" drill bit
- Scissors
- Fine file
- Diagonal cutters

Eventually, the plastic webbing on lawn chairs gives out and splits. Rather than re-webbing them, owners tend to throw them out and buy new ones. While the plastic may be shot, the aluminum tubing is usually in fine shape and ripe for reuse. With some quick cutting and drilling, a backyard accessory can be converted into a new and alternative one.

1. Disassemble the chair. Use the file and pliers to remove the rivets holding any brackets in place.

2. Using the tubing cutter, cut the tube portions of the chair into straight pieces. The goal is to cut 6 pieces of tubing from the chair ranging from approximately 10" to 18" long, with each tube 1½" longer than the previous one.

3. Look over the pieces of tubing you've cut from the chair frame and trim them into the required lengths while trying to avoid any holes or dents in the tubes.

4. Wear a dust mask for protection, and lightly sand and buff each piece using sandpaper or steel wool.

5. Drill a ⅛" hole through each tube, ½" from each end.

6. Drill a ⅛" hole through the center of the PVC pipe's end cap. Then drill pairs of holes around the edge of the cap at the positions for 12, 2, 4, 6, 8, and 10 o'clock. At each location, the pair of holes should be ¼" on center.

7. Using the fishing line and the hole you've drilled, suspend the tubes below the end cap.

71

8. Tie additional loops of line around the holes in the cap at 2, 6, and 10 o'clock. Above the cap, tie each of the remaining ends together at a single fishing swivel.

9. Tie an 8" length of line to the ring and tie the other end of the line to the other end of the swivel.

10. To make the clapper, tie one end of a 12" line to the bead, and pass the free end down through the hole in the center of the end cap. Drill a hole in the wood ball and slip it over the end of the line, then tie the end to the second swivel. Tie a 6" length of line to the other end of the swivel. Then, on the other end of that line, tie on the wind catcher. In this case, a silver fishing lure was used, but anything with some weight and some surface area will work.

11. Lastly, use the tubing cutter to tune the "chimes." Cut off a little bit at a time until each has a pleasing tone.

Tip The six pieces of tube here were cut from one lawn chair. Cutting up an aluminum chaise longue instead will generate longer pieces for a more dramatic look and deeper tones. You could use any kind of hollow metal object for a different look and sound.

Wine Crate Table

Time: 🕐   Skill: ⌄⌄⌄

Materials

- Hardwood (e.g. poplar) for:
  4 legs: 1" x 1" x 30"
  4 rails: 1" x 1", and the
  length needs to equal the
  widths of 3 crates + the
  width of 2 legs + 1"
  2 outer slats: 1" x 1" x 17¾"
  2 inner slats: ¾" x 3½" x
  17¾"
- Masonite for:
  2 side panels: ½" x 17¾" x
  height of the tallest crate
  + 1½"
  1 back panel: ½" x 17¾" x
  height of tallest crate + ½"
  1 base panel: ¼" x 17¾" x
  17¾"
- Scrap wood for guide strips:
  ⅜" x ⅜" x 17¾"
- Pine panel for tabletop
  2 x 4 ft
- #10 flathead wood screws
- Wooden knobs
- 4 rubber feet

  see over for tools . . .

This project was inspired by a tall credenza made up of old wine crates seen at a wine tasting.

You don't need to buy lots of vino to procure crates such as these. Just go to a well-stocked wine store and ask them nicely to save a few for you. Of course, you want the very prettiest (probably French) crates available. Here, the three wooden crates function as drawers. To expand the unit's storage potential, a shelf or one or two rows of drawers can easily be added below the top ones. It could form a very hip chest of drawers for a living room area or study.

All the wood remains unfinished and the screws are exposed to suit the raw quality of the crates. The concept is flexible and the wood thicknesses indicated are the minimum that will work, so play around with a design to match the crates you manage to get your hands on.

1. First, measure out and cut your wood and Masonite accurately, using the tape measure, combination square, and circular saw.

2. Construct the front and back frames as shown in Fig. 1, over the page. Pre-drill and install one #10 screw at each connection point. The distance between the top and bottom rail should be ½" more than the height of the tallest crate you have.

3. Pre-drill and screw the frames to the underside of the tabletop (see Fig. 2). The distance between the inside faces of each of the frames should equal the length of the slats.

4. Pre-drill and screw through the face frames to attach the slats. The inner slats should be centered on the gaps between the crates (see Fig. 3).

Wine Crate Table

Fig. 1

Fig. 2

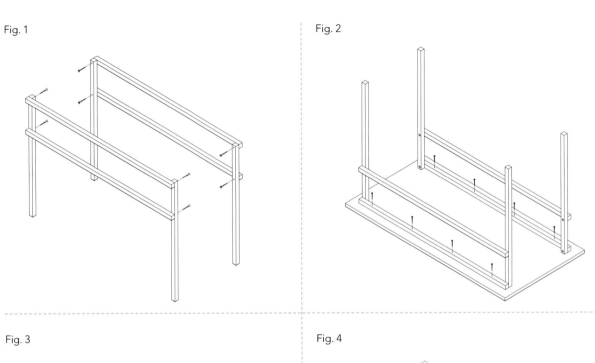

Fig. 3

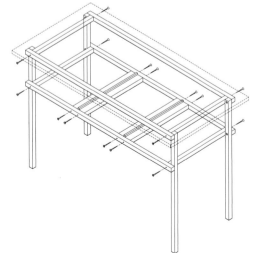

Fig. 4

Tools

- Pencil
- Combination square
- Tape measure
- Circular saw
- Electric drill with drill bits
- Screwdriver or screwdriver bit for drill
- Wood glue
- Sandpaper

5. Glue the bottom panel to the underside of the inner slats (see Fig. 4).

6. At this point, the legs will want to rack sideways a bit. Adjust the legs so that they are square to the tabletop and screw the back panel in place. Then screw the side panels in place. These panels serve to stiffen the table.

7. Glue the guide strips in place on top of the inner slats so that they will fit between the crates and allow each crate to slide out easily, forming a drawer.

8. Drill a hole in the front of each crate and attach the wooden knobs to the crates (see Fig. 5).

9. Screw a rubber foot onto the bottom of each leg. Your table is ready!

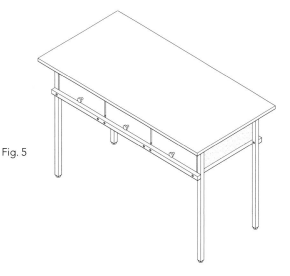

Fig. 5

Plastic Bag Dispenser

Materials

- Towel
- Thread
- Pins
- Safety pins
- Cotton cord
- Elastic cord

Tools

- Sewing machine

This is a dual reuse project. Not only can you recycle a towel or an old pants leg to make it, but once you put it into use, it gives you a convenient place to store all of your plastic grocery bags until you can reuse them. While it won't add much to your home's décor, it will help you make your kitchen or pantry a bit less cluttered.

1. Fold the towel lengthwise and sew a ¼" seam along the long edge, to within 1" from each end.

2. At one end, fold back into the cylinder 1" of fabric, and sew ¼" from the edge to form a hem. Leave both ends of the hem open.

3. Clip a safety pin through one end of the cotton cord and work it through the hem to create a drawstring. Remove the safety pin and tie the ends of the cotton cord together.

4. Roll a cuff on the other end of the cylinder about 1½" wide. Sew ¼" from the edge to form a wide hem. Leave a gap at each end of 1".

5. Clip a safety pin through the end of the elastic cord and work it through this hem. Once it's through, pull on the elastic so that the end of the cylinder puckers. Overlap the ends of the elastic 1" or so and stitch them to secure.

6. Tuck the ends of the elastic back into the cuff and stitch up the last bit of the hem.

7. Turn the whole thing inside out and you're ready to fill it with bags. Stuff them in through the drawstring end and pull them out one by one through the hole in the bottom end.

Tied Rag Basket

Materials

- Steel rod ³⁄₁₆" in diameter, 3 ft long
- 3 pieces ¼" wire mesh:
  1 piece: 34" x 13"
  2 pieces: 10" x 11"
- 8 old T-shirts
- Plywood or Masonite, ¼" x 9½" x 14"
- 14" x 18" piece felt
- 2 wood strips, ¾" x 1" x 8"
- Four 1" wood screws

Tools

- Vise or locking pliers
- Electrical tape
- Tin snips
- Straightedge
- Rotary cutter
- Cutting mat
- Bucket or bag
- Long tweezers
- Craft glue
- Electric drill with screwdriver bit

When the edges of a good T-shirt or polo shirt get too frayed it is usually retired to the rag bin, but instead it can go towards making this tied rag basket. It takes a lot of fabric to make a rag rug, but a basket such as this offers the look on a more manageable scale.

It's sized to hold folders, paperwork, or magazines and is strong because the structure of the basket is a simple box made out of ¼" wire mesh, with a frame of bent metal to stiffen the top edges. A felt-covered Masonite panel is used to stiffen the bottom.

To make the basket frame:

1. Clamp the steel rod in a vise and bend it to form a 10" x 13" rectangle. Position the bends so the ends of the rod meet in the middle of one of the short sides. Wrap the point where the ends meet with electrical tape. This completes the frame that will stiffen the open face of the basket.

2. Cut the large piece of mesh to size using the tin snips.

3. Bend the mesh into a "U" shape to create sides of 7" x 13" and a base of 10" x 13". Then fold the top two rows of mesh squares around the steel frame.

4. Cut the two smaller pieces of wire mesh to fit the two ends of the "U" shape, using the tin snips. Bend each of the short edges and one of the long edges so that the piece slips into the end of the basket. (Use the mesh squares as a guide to determine the best fit.) Then fold the top two rows of the side pieces over the metal frame. You'll have to snip a couple of squares out of the upper corners to make it bend neatly.

Tied Rag Basket

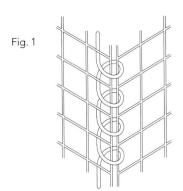

Fig. 1

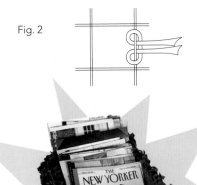

Fig. 2

To rag the basket:

5. Use the rotary cutter and straightedge to cut ⅜″ wide strips from the T-shirts. Each strip needs to be 3¾″ long. Mix up the colored strips really well in a basket afterward.

6. Cut four 12″ long pieces of T-shirt material to tie the corners of the mesh together. Loop a strip around two adjacent squares, pull tight, and draw the end of the strip down through the next square as shown in Fig. 1. Continue wrapping all the way down the edge and tie it off at the end. Do the same at all four corners.

7. Start at the upper right-hand corner of one side and loop one of the 3¾″ strips around the wire as shown in Fig. 2. Loop strips around all the vertical wires in the mesh and also around the top edge of the steel frame. A pair of long tweezers or a crochet hook can make this a bit easier.

To finish:

8. Cut the Masonite panel so that it fits into the base of the basket. Set the panel into the middle of the felt square. Fold the edges over on to the panel and glue in place.

9. Place the panel in the bottom of the basket, felt facing upward.

10. The wood strips are used as feet. Place one under each end of the basket. At each foot, drive two screws down through the bottom panel and into the top of the leg.

Variation: Tied Rag Rug

Use the same technique—and a lot more clothes—to create a rug. Instead of using the mesh to form a basket, simply cut a piece to the size you require and the attach the rags using the method above.

Window Sash Bookcase

Time: 🕐 **Skill:** ⋔⋔⋔

Materials

- 2 window sashes
- Plywood or MDF—sizing dependent on size of sashes
- 4 feet or casters
- Wood screws
- Wood glue
- ½" nails
- 1" finish nails
- Two 8 ft pieces of ½" x ½" x ⅟₁₆" aluminum angle
- Four 8 ft pieces of pine quarter round molding

see over for tools . . .

Using window sashes as sliding doors can liven up a basic bookcase. The key is to build the top, bottom, and sides extra deep to accommodate the thickness of the sashes.

The bookcase illustrated is a quick and basic version built from MDF, which is essentially recycled sawdust. Available in 4" x 8" sheets, it's inexpensive, very flat, and takes paint well. The downside is that it's heavy. The sashes were used as they were found, getting just a wash before they were installed.

The tracks in which the sashes slide are quite simple. The edges are strips of ½" quarter round molding and the middle divider is a length of ½" x ½" aluminum angle. The lengths and how far apart they are mounted will depend on the sashes you use.

The same basic idea can be applied to a more finished piece by repainting the sashes and using higher quality materials.

1. Obtain two window sashes, clean them, and paint them if desired.

2. Set them end to end and measure the overall width and length. Add ¼" to the shorter dimension and subtract 2" from the longer dimension. This will be the size of the back of the bookcase.

3. The sides are 18" wide and their height matches the height of the back. Also, cut a middle divider the same height and 9" wide.

4. The top and bottom are 18" wide and 3" longer than the back.

5. Cut the pieces to size and screw the back, sides, top, and bottom together to form a box. The back fits between the sides, which in turn fit between the top and bottom pieces. (The top and bottom should overhang the front and sides of the cabinet.) Then screw

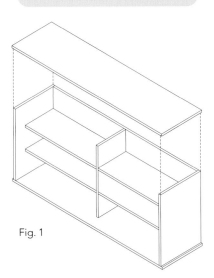

Fig. 1

Tools

- Tape measure
- Straightedge
- Combination square
- Power drill
- $\frac{1}{8}$" bit
- $\frac{1}{16}$" bit
- Countersink bit
- Screwdriver bit
- Pencil
- Sandpaper
- Circular saw or tablesaw
- Handsaw
- Hacksaw

the middle divider in place as shown in Fig. 1. For best results when working with MDF, predrill all of the holes and avoid driving a screw into the edge of the panels less than 2" from any corner.

6. Cut as many 9" wide shelves as desired and glue 9" long pieces of quarter round molding to the divider and sides to serve as shelf supports. Set the shelves in place.

7. Sand the edges of all the pieces.

8. Cut the quarter round and aluminum angle to match the length of the back panel of the bookcase. Drill a series of holes along one leg of the angle 18" apart using the $\frac{1}{16}$" bit.

9. Nail and glue the angle and quarter round to the top and bottom as shown in the cross section side view in Fig. 2. Install the innermost quarter round first. Then put a sash in place. Nail through the holes in the angles to fix them in place as shown in the diagram. Then set the second sash in place and install the outer quarter round. Leave enough space between the components to allow the sashes to slide. If they bind a little, lubricate the tracks with some paste wax.

10. Lastly, screw the feet or casters to the bottom of the cabinet. Depending on the length of your cabinet, an extra foot may be needed in the middle of the bottom to support the center of the cabinet.

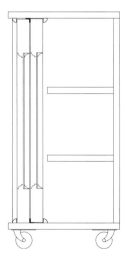

Fig. 2

Felt-Covered Table

Time: 🕐   Skill: ⋏⋏

Materials

- 1½ yd felt or other heavy fabric, such as cotton duck or twill
- Thread
- Pins
- Scrap double wall cardboard
- Packing tape
- Scrap wood for 4 legs, each 1" x 1" x 12"
- 4 rubber feet

Tools

- Tape measure
- Scissors
- Sewing machine
- Straightedge
- Pencil
- Utility knife
- Wood glue
- Screwdriver

Ever wonder why people buy expensive furniture only to hide it with slipcovers? Why not make a nice slipcover and put it over something cheap and simple?

That's the idea behind this table, which consists mostly of corrugated cardboard. The legs are lengths of scrap wood glued into a cardboard carcass, and to give the whole thing a tactile quality, the slipcover is made of felt. If the table wears out, you can recycle it and build a new one very easily.

The body of the table measures 14" x 14" square x 21" high, and for simplicity that's how we'll describe things here. Of course, you can adjust the measurements to build to a different design using the same materials. For best results, size the cardboard panels so that they fit inside your slipcover snugly. Keep in mind that it's easier to make the table fit the cover rather than make the cover to fit the table.

To make the slipcover:

1. Cut one piece of felt 57" long x 22" wide and a second piece 15" x 15" square.

2. Bring the two short ends of the long piece together to overlap each other by ¾". Pin and sew two lines of stitching along the overlap to fasten the ends together. You will have a large cylinder of felt. (See Fig. 1.)

3. Next add a bottom to the cylinder. Take the square piece of felt and position the middle of one of the edges against the end of the seam stitched in the cylinder, keeping right sides together. Pin the two together taking a ½" seam allowance. Then work your

Felt-Covered Table

Fig. 1

way along, pinning the two pieces together until the edge of the square is pinned to the edge of the cylinder.

4. Stitch along the line of pins, taking a ⅜" seam. Remove the pins.

5. Repeat steps 3 and 4 with each edge of the square of felt, until each side is sewn to the cylinder.

6. To finish, fold the edge at the open end of the cylinder over to the outside to make a ½" cuff. Pin and stitch ¼" from the edge to make a hem around the top edge of the bag.

7. Turn the bag inside out and it's done.

To make the box:

8. Cut a 14" x 14" square of cardboard for the top.

9. Cut two 21" x 14" pieces of cardboard for the side panels. Two further side panels should be cut 21" long and 14" wide but less twice the thickness of the cardboard. For example, if the cardboard is ¼" thick, then the width of the panel should be cut 13½" wide.

10. Cut eight 4" x 8" pieces of cardboard. The corrugations should run parallel to the short side. Score each strip lengthwise, down the middle, and fold the pieces into "L" shapes. For advice on scoring cardboard, see Techniques (page 139).

Fig. 2

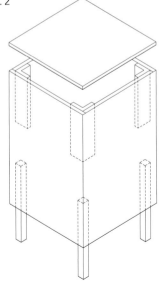

To assemble the table:

11. Carefully tape the long edges of the four side panels together to form a long tube. The wider sides should be placed opposite each other and should overlap the edges of the narrower panels. (See Fig. 2.)

12. Arrange the sides accurately and position the top to line up nicely on all four edges at one end. Tape the top panel in place, and where two pieces of cardboard meet at each edge, tape them completely. Before you go further, slide the slipcover over the box to make sure you're happy with the fit.

13. If all is well, flip the box over so you can reach the inside and glue the L-shaped pieces into the joint where the top meets the sides and where the sides meet each other. Avoid locating the L pieces where the legs will be attached.

14. Using a tape, measure and mark 14" up from the top panel in each corner. Now, glue the four wooden legs to the inside corners in the lower half of the box using the marks as the guide to ensure the table legs are level. Clamp the legs in place while the glue dries.

15. Once the glue dries and the legs are secure, screw the rubber feet onto the bottom of the legs. Flip the table over, slide the slipcover on, and smooth out any wrinkles.

Tip Cut a piece of ¼" thick plywood the size of the tabletop and lightly glue it to the top of the table before you put on the slip cover. This will provide some added durability and make it sound more substantial when you set a glass down on it.

Wine Cork Trivet

Materials

- Walnut wood strip 24" x 1½" x ¹⁄₁₆" (used in model making and available from hobby stores)
- Plastic tube or pipe 2" in diameter, 30" long
- Wood finish (such as tung oil or wax)
- Metal crate strapping ½" wide, 28" long
- Block of scrap wood
- Six ¼" grommets
- 75 wine corks

see over for tools . . .

It may take a while, or at least a few good parties, to accumulate sufficient corks to make a decent size trivet, but once you have, you can put them to work protecting your tabletop from hot dishes.

Two concentric bands hold the trivet together. The outer band, made from metal crate strapping, provides strength. The inner wooden ring stabilizes the corks. The two are held together with small grommets and the corks are held in place by friction when they are squeezed into the rings.

Metal strapping is used to secure cartons during shipping and your local lumber yard or home center is a good place to find some.

1. Trim the walnut wood strip to size using a utility knife and straightedge.

2. Plug the bottom of the plastic tube or pipe and wrap it well with duct tape. The idea is to make it watertight.

3. Run the kitchen faucet until the water is hot. Drop the wood strip into the tube and carefully fill the tube with hot water. The wood will want to float to the top, so push a pair of serving tongs or a bent coathanger into the tube to hold it down.

4. Stand the tube in the sink in case the bottom starts to leak and leave the wood in the water for 10 minutes or so until the water cools. It's important to keep the wood submerged, so if water does leak out, keep it topped up.

5. Remove the wood from the water and carefully wrap it around a cooking pot (see Fig. 1). Use the spring clamps or belt to keep the wood wrapped tightly around the pot and leave overnight to dry.

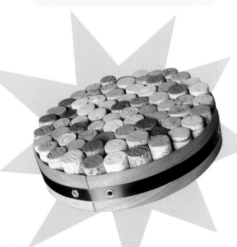

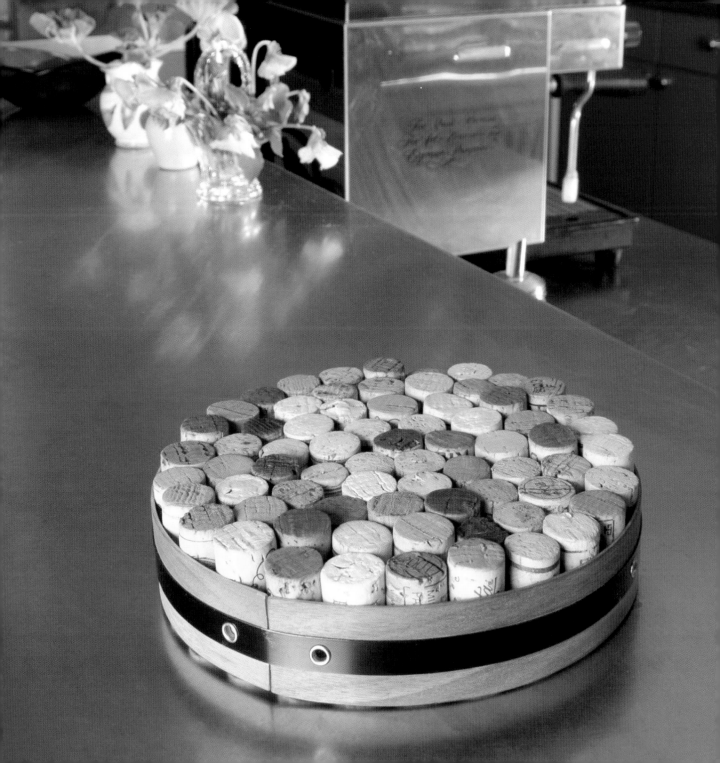

Tools

- Utility knife
- Metal ruler or straightedge
- Duct tape
- Cooking pot 8" in diameter
- Spring clamps or a wide web belt
- 220-grit sandpaper
- Masking tape
- Pencil
- Centerpunch
- Hammer
- Electric drilll with ⅛" and ¼" drill bits
- Grommet tool
- Awl
- Tin snips

6. Remove the clamps and slide the wood from the pot. You should have a nice wooden ring. Don't worry if the ends don't quite touch. If the wood is basically circular, it will work. Sand the wood and coat it with a finish such as tung oil or wax.

7. Wrap masking tape around the end of the metal strap. Make a mark in the middle of the strap about ½" from the end and make another mark 1½" further down.

8. Place the strap on a block of scrap wood and set the tip of the centerpunch on one of the marks you just made. Strike the punch with the hammer to create a dimple in the strap. Drill a ⅛" hole centered on the dimple, and then enlarge the hole using the ¼" bit. Repeat the process at the other mark.

9. Wrap the metal strap around the wood ring and tighten it until the ends of the wood touch (see Fig. 2). Ensure the ends of the metal strap with holes overlap on the outside. Mark the centers of these holes on the underlying end and drill these as before.

10. Wrap the strap again until the holes line up and slip one of the grommets through temporarily. Place the wooden ring inside the strap. The ends should just touch or slightly overlap. If they do overlap, trim one of the ends slightly.

11. Remove the wood and hold the looped strap in front of you with the pair of holes at 12 o'clock.

12. Unloop the strap and drill an identical pair of holes at 6 o'clock and a single hole at both 3 and 9 o'clock.

13. Install a grommet at the end of the strap, align the holes, and crimp it into place. Your strap is now a ring.

14. Insert the wooden ring inside the metal ring. The joint between the ends of the wood should be centered between the pair of holes you drilled at 6 o'clock. Adjust the metal ring so it's in the middle of the wooden ring (widthwise) and mark the centers of all the remaining holes on the wood ring.

15. Using the awl (or the tip of a nail or screw), make a dimple in the wood at all the marks you just make. (Don't use a hammer—just use hand pressure to avoid splitting the wood.) Drill the holes using the ¼" bit.

16. Wrap the wooden ring within the metal one and line up the holes. Crimp a grommet in each hole, locking the wooden and metal rings together.

17. Now start wedging the wine corks into the perimeter ring. At first the ring will be oval, but squish it a bit and try to rearrange the corks so they form concentric circles. Corks are slightly different sizes, so rearrange them until they all fit snugly. If a few are too long, trim them with a utility knife. The bits you slice off can be used as shims to wedge the corks tighter.

18. When all the corks fit tightly and you can lift the trivet without any falling out, you're done. Brew up a pot of tea and try it out.

Fig. 1

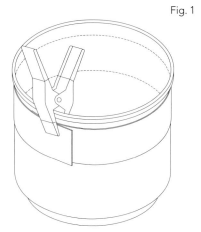

Fig. 2

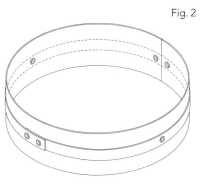

Tip The warmth of the hot water softens the fibers of the wood and makes them more pliable and willing to bend. Bigger pieces of wood used for furniture are cooked in steam boxes to achieve the same effect. In this case, the wood is thin so the hot water does the job. Sometimes the wood cracks in the process of bending, but don't be discouraged—it happens. Just try again with another piece.

Stone Drawer Pulls

Materials

- Aluminum tube, ³⁄₈" in diameter
- Attractive stones or pebbles, at least ⅝" thick
- Threaded rod, ⅛" in diameter
- Spacers
- Rubber washers, ¼" in diameter
- Metal washer to fit over rod
- Acorn nut to fit rod

Tools

- Tubing cutter
- Electric drill with ¼" masonry bit
- Hacksaw
- Fine file or fine steel wool
- Epoxy glue
- Small piece scrap wood
- Stick
- Baby oil
- Clamp

A beautiful accent to a plain piece of furniture can be the addition of some interesting hardware, and drawer pulls are a quick way to achieve this. Making your own gives the piece even more appeal, especially if it offers a way of bringing nature indoors.

Next time you're at the beach or on a hike, pick up a few interesting stones to use. Collect more than you think you'll need as some may be too hard to drill. Look for visible sedimentation lines in the stones as there's a good chance you can drill into this more easily.

1. Buff the aluminum tube and use the tubing cutter to trim off a piece ½" long.

2. Drill a ¼" hole approximately ³⁄₈" deep into the back of the stone.

3. With a hacksaw, cut off a piece of threaded rod. Note: the required length of the rod depends on the thickness of the drawer or door you are fitting. To determine the length, insert the rod into the stone and slide the spacer and washers over it as described in step 7. Then add the thickness dimension of the drawer plus an extra ⅛". Cut to size, and file any burrs from the ends.

4. Scrub the stone clean with a brush and water and let it dry thoroughly.

5. Mix some epoxy glue on a piece of scrap wood and use a stick to spoon it into the hole in the stone, filling it to about halfway.

6. Slowly insert the threaded rod into the hole, twisting and wiggling it to work out any air bubbles. Clean away any epoxy that gets on the stone as it will darken that area. Hold the rod in place until the epoxy cures. As it starts to stiffen, fine-tune the position of the rod, making it perpendicular to the back of the stone.

7. When the epoxy has cured, rub some baby oil into the surface of the stone to darken it and make its colors more visible. This will also help reduce staining from fingerprints.

8. Slip a rubber washer over the knob's threaded rod, then the aluminum spacer, and then another rubber washer. Slide the rod through the hole in the door or drawer front, then slide on the metal washer and thread the acorn nut onto the end to fix the whole thing in place. (See Fig. 1.)

Fig. 1

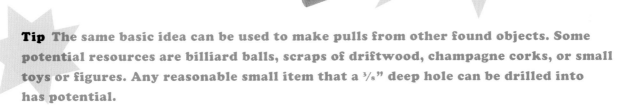

Tip The same basic idea can be used to make pulls from other found objects. Some potential resources are billiard balls, scraps of driftwood, champagne corks, or small toys or figures. Any reasonable small item that a ³⁄₈" deep hole can be drilled into has potential.

Junk Mail Pillows

Time: 🕐   **Skill:** ↖

Materials

- Large mailing envelopes
- Shredded paper
- Needle and thread

Tools

- Scissors
- Sewing machine
- Dowel or stick

For once, allow your junk mail to help bring you some relaxation instead of stress. Once you've shredded it, use it as filling for a throw pillow on which you can rest up before paying the real bills.

These steps will give you a rectangular pillow, but the same process can be used to make a free-form-shaped pillow. Just stitch a blob shape instead of a rectangle and then trim the excess envelope away, leaving about ½" of material beyond the stitch line.

1. Trim off the flap of the envelope.

2. Thread-stitch around the perimeter of the envelope, but stop short by 3" before the starting point to leave a gap in the stitching.

3. Snip the four corners off the envelope and then turn it inside out.

4. Stuff the envelope full of shredded paper, using a dowel or stick to get the stuffing into the corners. When it's fairly densely packed, sew up the 3" opening by hand.

Tip For best results, use spun polyester (Tyvek) envelopes for durability. A common source of these are the hard to tear (but seldom reusable) envelopes often used by courier companies.

Cardboard Tube Vases

Time: 🕐 | **Skill:** ꜛꜛ

Materials

- Cardboard tubes
- Sheet of paper
- Plastic or metal strapping
- Small grommets
- Plastic soda bottles
- Flowers

Tools

- Pencil
- Utility knife
- Sandpaper
- Tin snips
- Fine file
- Punch (for metal strapping) or awl (for plastic strapping)
- Masking tape
- Electric drill with drill bits
- Grommet tool

These vases are versatile. The short vase can sit on a table or hang from a hook on the wall, while the longer vase can hang from the wall with the flowers displayed out of its side. To display fresh flowers, insert a plastic container into the tube to hold water.

Cardboard tubes are used for packaging or as the cores in rolled products such as carpet, fabric and paper. Good sources are carpet companies, fabric shops, or reprographic shops.

The metal and plastic strapping used here can often be pulled out of the lumber racks at your local home center. (Avoid strapping that was wrapped around pressure-treated lumber, though.)

To make the short vase:

1. To cut the tube to the desired length, first make a cutting guideline. Wrap a sheet of paper around the tube so that the edges align all the way around, then mark onto the tube along the edge of the paper. Carefully score along the marked line with a utility knife, and keep working your way around the tube until it is cut through. For advice on scoring cardboard, see Techniques (page 139).

2. Using the scoring method again, cut two notches in the bottom of the tube slightly wider than the strapping.

3. Lightly sand the cut edges to even them out and remove any fuzzy bits.

4. Clean the strapping and cut it into manageable lengths using tin snips. Be careful, metal strapping is springy and cut edges can be sharp. Use a file to dull the sharp ends.

5. Cut a piece of strap long enough to wrap around the outside of the tube and allow the ends to overlap 1½".

6. Use an awl or punch to start a hole ⅜" from one end of the strap. Drill the hole large enough to accommodate the grommet. Metal straps are tough, so start by first drilling a small hole, and then enlarging it to the required size. It's also helpful to wrap the end of the metal straps with masking tape to make any marks you use to locate the holes easier to see.

7. Wrap the strap around the tube and find where the hole in the other end needs to be. The loop should be loose enough to allow a piece of strap to slip between it and the tube. Drill the second hole and then trim off the extra length.

8. Line up the holes and insert a grommet. Use the grommet tool to crimp it in place and lock the two ends together.

9. Determine how long you want the "J"-shaped strap to be and cut an appropriate length of strap. Drill a hole ⅜" from each end.

10. Make two bends in the strap to form a "J" shape. The short leg of the "J" runs up the front of the tube; the longer one runs up the back between the tune and the loop.

11. Slip the "J" and the loop into place around the tube and mark the spot on the front of the loop where the two intersect. Drill a hole in the loop, then grommet the two pieces together. Install a grommet in the hole at the other end of the "J."

12. Slip the tube into place.

13. Cut off the top of a plastic soda bottle, just below the neck, and slip this into the tube, to hold the water for your flowers.

To make the tall vase:

1. The long tube vase (right) is simpler to make than the shorter version. Start with a long tube and cut the "window" with a utility knife (see Fig. 1).

2. Drill a hole near the top end of the tube to use to hang it onto a wall hook.

3. Drill two pairs of holes to accommodate the rods as shown in Fig. 1. The upper rod helps support the stems. The lower rod supports a cut-off plastic bottle used to hold water and the flowers (as above). Use an interesting material for the rods; for example, pencils, twigs, bamboo, or scrap metal.

3. Pull the bottom rod out to remove or insert the water bottle.

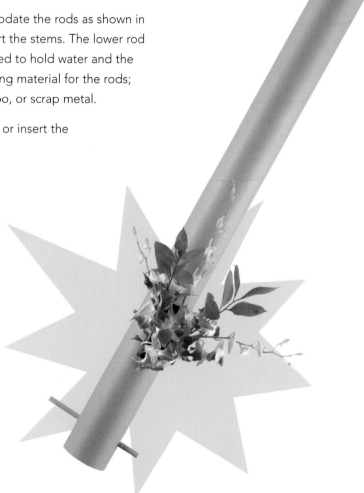

Fig. 1

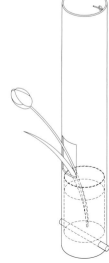

Mosaic Bowl

Time: 🕐   **Skill:** ↘

Materials

- Aluminum plate
- Magazines, brochures, or photographs

Tools

- Silver spray paint
- PVA glue
- Matte acrylic varnish
- Fine grade sandpaper

Old magazines and photographs can be used to create stunning mosaics that transform old objects. For this example, an old aluminum plate that was found in a dumpster was used, but you could use an old tray or something similar.

1. Clean the plate thoroughly, then paint the front of the plate using silver spray paint.

2. Cut up pictures from magazines, brochures, or old photographs into approximately ½" squares, choosing your color scheme before you start. This plate uses blues and turquoises, cut up from photographs of the sky and the sea in tourist brochures.

3. Glue the squares to the surface of the plate to create a mosaic effect.

4. To make the dish waterproof, apply 5–6 coats of matte acrylic varnish, sanding lightly using a very fine sandpaper after every two coats.

Tip To create a very interesting textured effect, you could cut up old architectural plans or maps instead of photographs. Alternatively, you could use pictures of wood samples to simulate a wood inlay.

Found Object Fruit Bowls

Time: 🕐	Skill: ⟍⟍

Materials

- Electric fan cover
- Rubber or cork coaster
- Stainless steel blender attachment
- Wok lid
- Stainless steel toilet roll holder

Tools

- Awl
- Nuts, bolts, and washers

Fruit bowls can be made using a variety of found objects. Inevitably, there will be several pieces of home and kitchen equipment lying around the house, or that you can easily scavenge, that no longer work. You can use old fans, blenders, woks, lids, or anything really, to create simple but stylish fruit bowls. These projects use an electric fan and a wok.

Electric Fan Bowl

1. The basic container of this fruit bowl was made using the cover of an electric fan that was no longer working. The base was made from a stainless steel blender attachment.

2. Cut a circle 3″ in diameter from a piece of rubber—you could use a rubber or cork coaster—and place it in the uneven depression in the center of the fan cover.

3. Punch a hole in the center of the rubber using an awl. Attach the base and wire cover using a nut and bolt suitable for the size of the hole, along with washers to hold everything together securely.

Tip Make sure the objects you choose are able to hold the weight of what you want to put in them. Be careful to balance the object on the base securely. Screw-in door handles or pot handles are good, and make an unusual object.

Found Object Fruit Bowls

Wok Lid Bowl

1. This fruit bowl started life as a lid for a wok. The base is an old stainless steel toilet roll holder with an attached pole.

2. Remove the handle from the wok lid, turn it around to the inside of the wok lid, and attach it to the base. This fruit bowl uses the knob from an old pressure cooker but you can use whatever you have lying about, even a door handle.

Tip To attach together items that have holes in the middle that are bigger then a typical screw head, use a fender washer on either side of the assembly to pinch the pieces together. Fender washers have a large outside diameter but a small inside diameter, and can bridge across a large hole. If an especially large washer is needed, create one by scrounging the lid of a metal tin or other container and drilling a hole in the center.

Zen Bamboo Lamp

Time: 🕐   **Skill:** 〜〜

Materials

- Old bamboo place mat
- 2 bamboo trivets
- Scrap of old fabric
- Metal strip with a hole in it to fit across the trivet
- Board pin or thumbtack
- Two small angle brackets
- Small piece of perforated metal sheet or thin plywood cut to size
- Needle and thread
- Screws, nuts, and bolts
- Adhesive spray or glue
      see over for tools . . .

Old bamboo place mats, combined with a bamboo trivet, make fantastic lamp shades as they filter the light in an interesting way. The trivets form the base and top of the light, while the place mat creates the lamp shade.

1. Measure around the inside of the trivet.

2. Cut the place mat across its length to the same size as the inside measurement of the trivet. The width of the mat forms the height of the lamp.

3. Glue the fabric to the mat to give the lamp its lining. Here a piece of material from an old blind was used. White fabrics work best as they diffuse the light.

4. Using the needle and thread, stitch the two edges of the mat to form a cylinder. Use simple straight stitches about 2" apart. For the most attractive result, the thread should match the color of the placemat. After the first few stitches, check that the completed cylinder fits the inside measurements of the trivet.

5. Secure the lined placemat to one of the trivets using a board pin. This will form the base of the lamp. Secure the second trivet to the other end of the mat to form the top.

6. Mark a point on the inside of each face of the lamp ½" from the top and bottom edge. Use the awl to make a hole at this point.

7. Secure the mat to the inside of the trivets using small screws.

8. Using a handsaw, cut a square piece of wood sized to slip inside the base of the lamp. Drill a $\frac{1}{2}$" diameter hole in the center of the square and glue the strips to the bottom of the square along opposite sides. This should give you someting that looks like a little table with a hole in the middle. Glue it into the bottom of the lamp shade with the "legs" facing down.

9. Follow the instructions on page 38 to wire the lamp. Thread a 1 $\frac{1}{4}$" piece of lamp rod into the base of the socket.

10. Lastly, put the end of the cord through the hole in the base of tthe lamp, insert the rod through the hole, thread a nut onto the end and then install a plug on the end of the cord. Remember: When you turn it on for the first time keep an eye on the shade to make sure it stays cool enough, and use a small low wattage bulb to avoid overheating the shade.

Tip Two identical wooden picture frames (without glass) would make a good substitute for the trivets. Or you could scrounge some wood to make a pair of simple wood frames. You could also try following the wood bending instructions on page 90 to make a pair of matching wood rings rather than squares, which would create a round lamp. An old wooden blind could be trimmed and used to make the lamp shade instead of the place mat.

Record Album Mail Organizer

Time: 🕐   **Skill:** ⌇⌇

Materials

- 4–6 record albums
- Small grommets or rivets

Tools

- Iron and ironing board
- Old T-shirt
- Gloves
- Cardboard or wooden tube such as packaging roll or small rolling pin, 1½" in diameter, at least 18" long
- Grommet tool
- Spring clamps or binder clips

It's easy to find some really awful record albums at garage sales and thrift stores. Changes in technology aside, their content alone is reason enough to assume that they'll never be played again. So why not sacrifice a few in the name of home décor?

The first step is to bend the records. The organizer in the photo uses four records. You'll need a couple of extra ones for practice first, though.

1. Heat the iron to "high." Slip the record inside an old T-shirt and place it on the ironing board. Run the iron over the T-shirt and record for 20–30 seconds, moving it slowly the entire time. Focus on a line tangent to the record's label. The goal is to soften this area enough to allow it to bend while leaving the rest of the disk stiff and flat.

2. When the time is up, put on the gloves, as the record will be very hot. Quickly pull the record out of the shirt and wrap the softened area around the tube to form it into a "U" shape.

3. When you have four nicely bent records, stack them as shown in the photo and use three grommets or rivets to join each album to its neighbor.

4. Once they are all fastened together, hang the unit on a nail in the wall, using the spindle hole of the top record. Now you have a hip organizer for sorting your mail and you never need to listen to those ghastly old records again.

Tin Can Pen Rack

Materials

- Aluminum rod, ½" in diameter, 24" long
- 5 identical cans
- Thick black hair elastics (buy the longest ones you can find)
- Pushpins (long length and with aluminum heads work best) or nails

Tools

- Tubing cutter or hacksaw
- Steel wool

If you peel away the label and objectively consider the common can, the ribbed, polished surface is actually rather pleasing.

This is one of the simplest projects in the book. If you already have a dowel or rod the right length, no tools are required. A ½" diameter aluminum tube is pictured, but any stiff rod, tube, dowel, or even a reasonably straight stick of roughly the same diameter will do the job.

1. Use the tubing cutter, cut the aluminum tube to length. (A hacksaw will also work, but you'll have to file the cut ends to remove any burrs. The tubing cutter does a quicker, cleaner job.)

2. Buff the surface of the rod with the steel wool for a nice shine.

3. Clean the cans well and remove the labels and glue. Stubborn glue can be removed with a bit of WD-40 or other solvent.

4. Loop the elastics around the cans and the tube as shown in Fig. 1. The elastics should rest in the ribs of the cans.

5. Loop two more elastics around the rod to use as hanging points.

6. Push two pushpins or hammer two fine nails into your wall far enough apart to line up with the hanging loops.

7. Hang the assembly on the pins and fill the cans with your pens, pencils, markers, and whatever else will relieve the clutter on your desk. You can even insert a note, photo, or sheet of paper between the wall and the bottom edges of the cans, which will stay in place by friction alone.

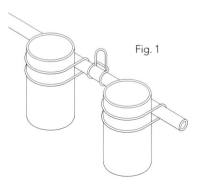

Fig. 1

CD Case Photo Display

Time: 🕐 **Skill:** ↖

Materials

- 2 aluminum channels, 4 ft long with an inside width of ½"
- Heavyweight illustration board
- CD cases
- Photos, found art, news clippings, colored paper
- 3 flathead wire nails

Tools

- Tape measure
- Hacksaw
- Fine file
- Straightedge
- Pencil
- Utility knife
- Steel wool
- Silicone sealant
- Caulk gun
- Hammer

No one has a shortage of CD cases after converting their music to MP3 format. And it seems such a shame to throw them out. This project puts them to use in an easily changeable, modular photo display.

Vary the look by adding colored paper or found art rather than just photographs. The example opposite is 4 ft long; a longer version would be a great way to dress up a hallway and an excellent way to display many of your favorite snapshots or trimmed postcards.

1. Take an extra piece of the aluminum channel and a CD case with you when you buy the illustration board. Choose board thick enough to fit snugly into the channel behind the case yet thin enough still to allow the cases to slide out. See Fig.1a and 1b, on the next page, for how the three materials should fit together.

2. Cut the channels to the desired length. Use a file to remove any burrs from the cuts and buff with steel wool until the aluminum shines.

3. Use the utility knife and straightedge to cut the illustration board into sufficient strips to give a length that is 8" shorter than the channels and ⅛" wider than the CD cases. Line them up end to end.

4. Run a bead of silicone along the inside edge of the channels. (The stuff you use to caulk around your bathtub is fine.) Slip the edges of the board into the channels and press them down into the sealant.

CD Case Photo Display

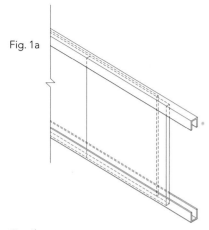

Fig. 1a

Fig. 1b

5. Once the board is in place and the ends of the channels line up with each other, slide the CD cases into the channels to ensure the board is bedded well in the silicone. The cases will wedge things in place as the silicone cures. Make sure no excess silicone is oozing out and gluing the cases in place.

6. Prepare the artwork and trim it to size. Pop the CD cases apart and remove the insert that clips the CD in place. Insert the artwork into the back face of the case, then reinstall the insert and the cover.

7. When the silicone is cured, hang the frame on the wall by nailing through the illustration board. Slip the CD cases into the ends of the channels.

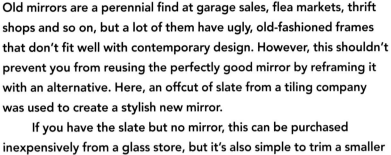

Slate Tile Mirror

Time: 🕐   **Skill:** ↖↖

Materials

- Offcut of slate
- Mirror
- Picture hook and nail
- Tacks
- Felt

see over for tools . . .

Old mirrors are a perennial find at garage sales, flea markets, thrift shops and so on, but a lot of them have ugly, old-fashioned frames that don't fit well with contemporary design. However, this shouldn't prevent you from reusing the perfectly good mirror by reframing it with an alternative. Here, an offcut of slate from a tiling company was used to create a stylish new mirror.

If you have the slate but no mirror, this can be purchased inexpensively from a glass store, but it's also simple to trim a smaller piece out of a broken mirror that has been discarded. A glasscutter, some oil to lubricate the cutter wheel, and a straightedge are all the tools that are necessary.

1. Use the square, straightedge, and marker pen to draw the cut marks on the piece of slate. Remember that the hole in the frame should be slightly smaller than the size of the mirror. Using the sharp point of a tile cutter, score the surface as deeply as possible. Then, with bevelled side down, use a bricklayer's trowel to chop the edge.

2. If you need to cut the mirror to size, use the square, straightedge, and marker pen to lay out the cut marks on the mirror so that the trimmed piece will fit into the frame with just a little room to spare. Cut the mirror or board with the glasscutter or saw, insert it into the frame, and press some map pins into the frame behind it to hold everything in place.

117

Slate Tile Mirror

Tools

- Fine-tip marker pen
- Square
- Straightedge
- Tile cutter
- Trowel
- Glasscutter
- Household oil
- Handsaw or circular saw
- Hammer
- Map pins

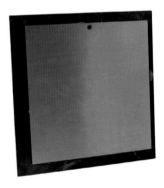

3. As the wheel of the cutter is rolled along the straightedge, it etches a line in the surface of the glass, weakening it at that point. The scored line is then aligned with a table edge and flexed. With a bit of luck, the glass should break cleanly along the line you just scored. (Note that glass dust is created when glass is etched and it's good to have a damp paper towel handy to wipe it up.)

4. Back the mirror with some cardboard and then cut a piece of strong cloth such as felt to slightly larger than the size of the mirror. Glue the felt to the slate frame to hold the mirror in place.

Variation: Slate Place Settings

If you have scraps of slate that aren't large enough to make a frame, use them to create personalized place settings for your dinner parties. Either cut the pieces of slate to the required size using the technique in step 1, or leave them as you found them for a more interesting shape. Write the names of your guests on the slate in chalk before you set the table. You could even write out the whole menu so your guests know what they have to look forward to. And the best bit? They're totally recyclable—simply wipe clean ready for your next party.

Tip You can also use the slate to make a stylish picture frame, or anything else that springs to mind. Or you can use a different kind of tile—it doesn't have to be slate.

Carry Along Cushions

Time: 🕐   **Skill:** ↖

Materials

- Rice sack
- Old cushion

Tools

- Scissors
- Needle and thread

Empty rice sacks can easily be turned into cushions that will really brighten up your sofa or garden chairs. Alternatively, the handles on the bag mean you can carry the cushion around with you to picnics or to the beach. You can even take the cushion out and fill the bag up with shells, stones, or anything else you want to collect while you're out and about.

No-Sew Version

1. Take an empty rice sack and the cushion pad out of an old cushion or pillow that you don't use any more.

2. Push the cushion inside the bag. If the bag has a zip, as with the white cushion, all you need to do is zip the bag up and your cushion is ready to go.

Needle and Thread Version

1. If your rice sack doesn't have a zip, as in the yellow cushion, you can sew the top of the bag shut.

2. Alternatively, make a cut in the center of each of the handles. Then tie the two sides of the cushion together using the handles. A bow looks prettier, but you can use a knot if the handles are too short.

Tip If you want to make a waterproof cover for cushions you can use in the garden, use one of the bigger, waterproof sacks or bags on the market. Some of them have interesting colors and text, ranging from advertisements to film posters.

Decoupage Tray

Materials

- Printers' tray
- Text or image to lay over the tray
- Felt or plastic backing

Tools

- Fine grade sandpaper or wet and dry sandpaper
- Plastic wood or putty
- Acrylic primer
- Paint
- Fixative such as glue
- Gold leaf
- Varnish

Decoupage is the process of finishing or decorating an object by gluing colored or printed paper to it and then applying coats of a clear sealer until the surface feels smooth. In this case we've brought to life an old printers' trays from a flea market, but the same technique can be applied to larger items such as old bland furniture.

The inspiration for using the script came from the fact that the tray was originally used to store metal types and fonts for printing. The paper you use in your project can also play on the item's former life, or not. Be creative!

1. Remove any knobs or buttons from the tray. Clean the tray thoroughly and, when it is dry, smooth and sand it.

2. Fill any holes with plastic wood or putty and sand the tray again to create a smooth surface.

3. Prepare the tray using an acrylic primer.

4. Paint a base coat of red acrylic paint and leave to dry, then apply another coat.

5. There are many ways of finishing the tray. To copy the script tray, enlarge and photocopy in black and white a page of script slightly smaller than the tray, leaving a ½" red border when you glue the paper to the tray.

6. Brush a used tea bag over the photocopy to give it an aged look and allow it to dry, then use a fixative spray to seal the image.

7. Place gold leaf randomly over the script and the edges of the tray.

8. Apply 5–6 coats of matte water-based acrylic varnish to the entire tray, alternating the direction of strokes on each layer.

9. Sand with fine grade sandpaper or wet and dry sandpaper after the first three coats and before the last coat of varnish, wiping with a dry cloth after each sanding. Leave the varnish to dry thoroughly before applying each layer of varnish. Seal the piece with a last coat of varnish.

10. To finish the tray, cut a piece of felt or cloth the same size as the tray and fix it to the bottom of the tray. In this case plastic backing, which was originally from a rice sack, was used. A roll of 1″ cork strip found in a scrap bank was then glued onto the tray to form a border. Felt can be used instead of cork.

Variation: Decoupage Table Top
Use the same technique to create a stunning table top, following the same technique as for the tray.

Tip Any kind of image, text, or print could be used to finish the tray, including newspaper, notepaper, or magazines. Instead of using a cloth or plastic backing for the underside you can use a primer and two coats of acrylic paint. Four felt pads can be fixed to the four corners to protect the table surface. In a similar way, drawers from old tables and kitchen units—or old trays—can be given a quick and dramatic facelift.

Slide Show Light Feature

Time: 🕐 **Skill:** ⟍

Materials

- Cable junction box
- $\frac{3}{32}$" x 3" wide wood sheets (available at craft and hobby stores)
- Scrap cardboard or mat board
- Slides
- 2 scrap wood blocks
- Nuts and bolts
- Slim fluorescent strip light
- Scrap plexiglass

Tools

- Electric drill
- Gel-type Krazy glue
- Utlity knife
- Pencil
- Straightedge
- Plexiglass knife

You can make interesting objects from bits of architectural salvage, for instance, an electrical panel or cable junction box, which are often discarded when offices renovate. They are used to hide cables along the walls of buildings, but you can use a box and some old slides to make a great light feature.

Use pictures of your family, holiday, or anything you find interesting. It is designed to be easily taken apart, so you can change the images to keep things interesting—or to redecorate your home.

1. Clean the cable junction box thoroughly. Drill two holes in the back of the junction box to correspond to the holes in the strip light housing.

2. Cut two wood blocks to fit snugly into the ends of the junction box while leaving a $\frac{3}{8}$" gap between the block and the back of the box for air circulation.

3. Fit the blocks to the ends of the box and measure the space between them. This is the space you have available to display your slides.

4. Cut two pieces from the wood sheet with a utility knife. The measurements are determined as follows: First measure the height of the slides and the width of the junction box. Subtract the height of the slides from the width of the junction box and divide the result by two. Add $\frac{1}{4}$" to allow for some overlap.

5. Cut two more strips from from thin wood or cardboard, using the same length measurement as before but $\frac{1}{4}$" narrower. Make sure the wood or cardboard is at least as thick as the slides.

125

6. Cut a piece of transparent plexiglass (⅛" thick minimum) to match the inside width of the box. The length should match the length of the wood strips you just cut.

7. Glue the narrower slats to the face of the plexiglass, one along the top edge and one along the bottom. Make sure the slides fit between the two strips before the glue dries. Then glue the wider strips to the tops of the narrow strips, again aligning the edges.

8. Glue one block into the end of the junction box to prevent the slides from falling out.

9. Insert the plastic and wood panel into the box and hold it tight against the lips along the top and bottom edges of the box. Inside the top and bottom of the box, glue strips of wood in place to hold the panel against the lips. Take care not to accidentally glue the panel into place as well. You want to be able to slide it out to change the lightbulb.

10. Attach the strip light in place.

11. To finish, slot your slides into place in front of the plexiglass. Insert the remaining wood block in the open end of the box and turn the light on.

Tip If you don't have a cable junction box, you could use some other architectural salvage such as metal wall studs or gutters. And instead of using store-bought wood, consider using the slats from a discarded wooden window blind, as we used here.

Candy-Wrapper Bowl

ACCESSORY

Time: 🕐   **Skill:** ⬈

Materials

- Candy wrappers

Tools

- Needle and thread

Collect the foil coverings of chocolate and candy wrappers and use them to create a shimmering bowl.

1. Start by twisting one foil wrapper into a tight roll. Connect the next wrapper to it by twisting the ends together to create a rope.

2. When the candy-wrapper rope is about 2 ft long, form one end into a small circle. Using a needle and some strong thread (you could cut a long thin strip from a plastic bag), stitch the circle together.

3. Next, create a second candy-wrapper rope about 10 ft long and start attaching it to the inner circle. Secure each stitch by looping the thread around the needle and pulling it. Use simple stitches (or a blanket stitch) and form a tight spiral, coiling the foil rope to create a bowl shape.

4. Attach two rows of coils of the same size to the bottom of the bowl to make a stand.

Variation: Plastic Bag Coasters

Use the same technique to create colorful coasters out of plastic bags. Twist the bags together using the same technique as for the foil wrappers, making sure to use a variety of different colors, and stitch together to form a circle. The advantage of using plastic bags is that the coasters will be waterproof, so you won't ruin them if you spill your drink.

Night Stand

Materials

- 1 piece of wood 1" x 4" and 4 ft long (or 4 scraps at least 12" long)
- 1 cutting board, wood or plastic, at least 14" x 15"
- ⅛" thick clear plexiglass at least 13" x 14"
- Mat board at least 12" x 12"
- 1 piano hinge 12" long with screws
- 2 self-adhesive furniture feet ⅛" thick
- 2 high-strength magnets (from stationery store)
- 2 keyhole hooks
- 4 shelf pins
- 8 screws 1½" long min
- 4 screws ⅜" long max
- Wood glue

see over for tools . . .

By day, these little drop-front cabinets appear to be simple photo frames. But at night they open to serve as bedside tables. In other situations, they could also work as end tables or, turn one 90 degrees and use it as a key cabinet near your entry.

These tables are not very large: 16" by 16" is about a big as you want to go to avoid overstressing the hinge. The 1 x 4 lumber used here is 3½" wide and will make a cabinet deep enough to hold a Kleenex tissue box lying on its side. Other than that, the dimensions are flexible and may be adjusted based on the materials available.

1. Cut two pieces of wood 9½" long for the top and bottom and two pieces 12" long for the sides.

2. Drill a pair of holes part way through each side to accommodate the shelf pins. Alternatively, glue on two slim strips of wood or metal to support the shelf.

3. Arrange the top and bottom pieces between the sides to form a rectangular box

4. We used a plate joiner to make a concealed connection at each of the corners, but using a pair of screws to join each corner will work just as well. Just remember to pre-drill the screw hole to prevent the wood from splitting. In any case, be sure to use some sort of mechanical connection here for strength. Don't rely on wood glue alone.

5. Once the wood pieces are joined, you have the frame of your cabinet and it's time to install the keyhole hooks. These hooks will slide over the head of a screw in the wall and drop down over it,

Tools

- Electric drill
- Variety of drill bits
- Scrap wood to put under work-piece when drilling
- Sandpaper
- Circular saw
- Plexiglass knife
- File
- Hacksaw
- Pencil
- Tape measure
- Square
- Utility knife
- Straightedge
- Small and large screwdrivers

securely holding the cabinet in place. Before you attach the hook plate to the cabinet, drill out some wood beneath it to provide clearance for the screw head. You can then put the plate on. Locate it about quarter of the way from the top of the cabinet.

6. If you plan to paint or clear-coat the cabinet, do so now.

7. Cut the mat board to a size large enough to cover the back of the cabinet. The hooks will prevent the mat from lying flat on the wood, so cut notches in the sides of the mat to clear them. Once it fits nicely, glue the mat to the back of the cabinet frame.

8. If necessary, trim the cutting board to size. Ideally, it should overlap the cabinet by 1" or so on the top and sides and 3" at the bottom. The 3" overlap at the bottom helps to support the tabletop when it is in the down position. If you trim a plastic cutting board, use a file to smooth the cut edges.

9. Using the plexiglass knife, cut the plexi to a size a bit smaller than the final dimensions of the cutting board.

10. While your tools are out, cut a piece of plexi or one of the cutting board scraps to use as a shelf in the cabinet.

11. On the cutting board, draw a line 3" from one of the short edges. Line the barrel of the hinge up with this mark with the leaves pointing toward the edge you measured from. Screw the hinge in place using all of the screw holes available. To get a hinge the right length, you may have to use a hacksaw to cut a longer hinge down to size. If so, locate your cuts to maximize the number of screw holes in the leaves of the hinge.

12. Place the cutting board over the face of the cabinet and unfold the hinge so that the free leaf is against the bottom of the cabinet. Then screw that leaf in place.

13. Stick two rubber furniture pads to the bottom of the cabinet. These will act as shims to keep the tabletop level when it is in the down position.

14. With the cutting board/tabletop in the closed position, center the plexiglass on the surface that will be the underside of the table. Drill four holes through the plexi into the cutting board. Put your photo under the plexi and screw it in place using the holes you just drilled.

15. To make a catch to hold the cutting board in the closed position, use a pair of magnets. Flip the tabletop open and drill a hole in the face of the top of the cabinet. Glue one of the magnets into the hole. Locate the matching spot on the tabletop and do the same for the second magnet. Before you glue it in though, make sure its polarity is facing the right way!

16. To hang the nightstand, measure the distance between the centers of the keyhole hooks and mark those locations on the wall. Install two screws in the wall that have heads small enough to fit into the hooks. Be sure to use wall anchors to prevent the screws from pulling out of the wall.

17. When your project is mounted, set the shelf in place. Stand back, admire your work, and go stock up your night stand with whatever you need for the night!

Techniques

Drilling Holes

GENERAL RULES
- Wear eye protection. Make sure hair, clothing, and jewelry are pulled back and secured to avoid snagging or tangling.
- Don't advance the bit too quickly. When drilling hard or brittle material like plastic, it is helpful to start the hole with a small bit and work up to the final size bit.
- Drill bits can get hot during drilling, especially if they are dull or if you are making a large hole. Back the drill out of the hole periodically to help eject shavings and allow the bit to cool.

1. First, mark the location of the hole on your work piece. If you have multiple holes to make, it is most efficient to do all the layout work at once.

2. Use an awl or center punch to mark the center of the hole. This makes a little divot for the tip of the drill bit to rest in, which helps keep it accurately located and prevents it slipping to the side as you begin to drill.

3. If the work piece is small, clamp it to the bench top or hold it securely in a vise. If you intend to drill all of the way through the material, place a piece of scrap wood beneath the hole to avoid drilling into the bench. This will also prevent your work piece from splintering (see Fig. 1).

4. Select a drill and bit based on the size and depth of the hole and the material you'll be drilling into. Insert the bit into the chuck of the drill and tighten it so that the bit is held securely.

5. Place the tip of the drill bit on the center mark that you made with the awl and hold the drill so the bit is perpendicular to the work surface. From whatever direction you look at it, it should not look tipped. If it does, the hole will be made through the work piece at a skewed angle (see Fig. 2).

6. Most electric drills have a variable speed trigger which works like the gas pedal on a car— the harder you press, the faster it goes. As you start drilling, the motor should run relatively slowly. Once the hole is established, you can increase the speed. When the hole reaches full depth, keep the motor running and pull the bit from the hole. Don't stop the drill with the bit in the hole—it may bind, and be tough to remove.

With that, the hole is complete.

Fig. 1

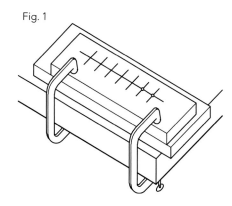

Fig. 2

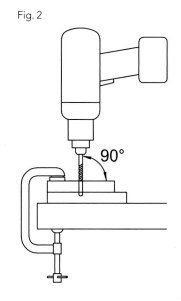

Clamping/Holding

Without a sturdy base on which to work and a secure means to hold a piece of work, it is difficult to obtain the best results. To avoid frustration and for safety's sake, it is important to support a work piece during each step of fabrication, repair, or assembly.

GENERAL RULES
- Ensure the work piece will be adequately supported throughout the entire process.
- Keep clamping surfaces clear and clean, as debris can damage the surface of a work piece.
- Place scraps of wood between the work and the jaws of a clamp or vise to distribute the pressure and to avoid scratching, denting, or discoloring the work piece.
- Assemble your project beforehand without the use of glue or fasteners, to ensure all the pieces fit properly. Use this opportunity to decide how many clamps you willl need and where they will be positioned.
- Arrange the clamps on the work piece to apply pressure evenly.
- Do not use a clamp or vise to force objects together. If they do not mate properly, find out why and correct the problem.

Clamps are available for almost any size project. Below is a brief overview of the common types (see Fig. 1 and 2):

SPRING CLAMPS
These work like large clothes pins. They don't exert much pressure, but can be applied and removed quickly using only one hand.

C-CLAMPS
Many different sized C-clamps are available, but those between 1 and 6 inches are most common. Their strong, rigid frames mean they can deliver a large amount of pressure to a small area.

PARALLEL JAW CLAMPS
The broad surface area of their jaws distributes pressure more evenly and that, combined with their wooden jaws, makes them less likely to dent or mar a woodwork piece.

BAR CLAMPS
These are used for clamping larger projects like drawers or boxes. Their maximum capacity depends on the length of the bar. Clamps with bars from 6" to 36" long are available.

PIPE CLAMPS
Pipe clamps are similar to bar clamps except that they can be made much longer (up to several feet) since they use stiff steel pipe as the "bar." The clamping mechanism will also deliver more pressure than the smaller, lighter bar clamps. This makes pipe clamps suitable for very large projects such as furniture and cabinetry.

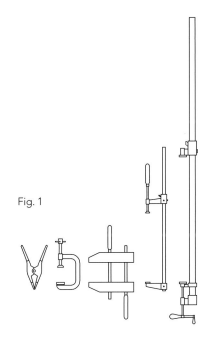

Fig. 1

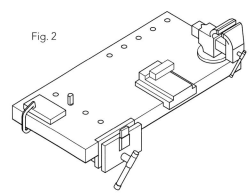

Fig. 2

Using a Glasscutter

A glasscutter doesn't really cut the glass. It just scores the surface so that you can break it in a controlled way. The glass will tend to fracture along the line of weakness created by the score, which is created by drawing the cutter across the glass along a straightedge, as you would when cutting something with a utility knife.

GENERAL RULES
- When the cutter rolls across the glass, it leaves a trail of glass dust behind. Have a damp paper towel on hand to wipe this up.
- Work on top of some sheets of newspaper to catch any stray glass splinters.
- Wear eye protection when scoring and snapping the glass.

First you need to do some prep work. Clean the glass well and make sure it is free of grease, and lubricate the cutting wheel well so that it rolls, rather than slides, on the glass. When you use the cutter, expect to hear a grinding noise.

Use your straightedge to mark where you need to score. Score the full width of the glass and lighten your pressure as you reach the end of the cut so you don't chip the edge.

Flip the glass over and use the ball on the end of the cutter to gently tap the glass behind the score to weaken it. Flip the glass back over, align the score with a table edge or with a strip of wood on the table top, and flex the glass. The glass should break along the score line. If the break isn't straight, hook one of the notches in the cutter over the remaining bits to nibble them back to the score line. An oilstone can be used to dull the sharp edge of the glass.

Scoring Cardboard

When you score, cut the cardboard but don't go all the way through so the skin of one side of the cardboard acts as a hinge. Practice on some scrap pieces first to get a feel for how deep you need to cut to score rather than sever right through.

Cutting with Blades

The quickest and cleanest way to cut many thin materials is with a knife, rather than with scissors or some type of saw. In each situation, the same basic techniques apply. First, a few words about the tools available.

Hobby knives generally have small pointed blades that clamp into pen-like handles. These are best reserved for fine-scale or detail-oriented work. Longer cuts and thicker materials are usually better dealt with by utility knives, of which there are two basic types. Sheet rock knives have replaceable trapezoid-shaped blades that are stiff and strong, which makes them suitable for heavy-duty cutting. The other type has a long blade housed in the handle that can be advanced and broken off in increments as the tip dulls. These make good all-purpose knives and will work well for most of the projects in the book that call for a knife.

Rotary cutters are used in a manner similar to knives, but rather than dragging the edge of a blade across a surface, the cutter has a round blade that rolls across. These are very sharp and can only be used to cut fabric and paper, but do an excellent job at it.

Long, straight cuts are best accomplished by cutting along a straightedge. Steel, aluminum, and plastic straightedges are available. The best general-purpose edge is a cork-backed steel ruler. The cork helps prevent the ruler from slipping during the cut and the knife will not dig into the steel, which can occur with aluminum or plastic straightedges if they are not used carefully. In fact, plastic straightedges are generally to be used only with rotary cutters.

Also, something should be placed beneath the cut to avoid marring the work surface. Scrap cardboard will work in a pinch, but purchasing a self-healing cutting mat from a craft store is a wise investment. It's cheaper than a new dining room table…

GENERAL RULES
- Measure out where the cut needs to occur, then set the material on the cutting mat, making sure the cut won't run beyond the mat.
- Align the straightedge with the marks and hold it firmly in place, keeping your fingers well away from the edge along which the knife will travel.
- Act out the cut beforehand, making sure nothing important is in the way if the knife were to slip.
- Draw the knife along the edge with a medium pressure. It's better to make a few passes with the knife than try to cut all the way through in one shot.

Using Tin Snips

Tin snips are large, heavy-duty scissors with short, deep cutting edges. They are available in lengths ranging from 7" to 16". There are three types of tin snips, distinguished by colored handles. Yellow indicates a shear capable of making a straight-ahead cut, and cuts to the right or left; red indicates a straight-ahead cut, or a cut curved to the left; green indicates a straight-ahead cut, or a cut curved to the right. Red- and green-handled shears can cut tighter curves than yellow-handled types.

GENERAL RULES
- Long handles give good leverage to cut through thick materials.
- For more control, you can clamp one handle of the snips in a bench vise, allowing you to concentrate on guiding the material through the shears.
- When buying these tools, look for smoothly operating shears that have well-forged components.
- You can sharpen a used pair of tin snips by clamping them in a vise and filing the edge to an 85° angle.

To cut a tight outside curve or circle with straight-bladed shears or snips, nibble away until you achieve the shape you need.

Keep the cutting edge of the tool perpendicular to the sheet metal, otherwise the tool can slip sideways and wedge between the cutting jaws, fouling the work and the tool.

Resources

www.mcmaster.com
An industrial supply house that stocks so much stuff you could probably build your own space station and furnish it. It's a good place to look for unusual hardware and is chockful of informative little primers on various products and materials.

www.freecycle.org
Rather than putting usable items in the trash, people post them here to give other people a chance to claim and use them.

www.rockler.com
A broad selection of woodworking tools and unusual hardware.

www.sciplus.com
American Science and Surplus with lots of odd surplus goodies for inspiration.

www.craigslist.com
Free online want ads.

www.readymademag.com
A great magazine for people who like to make stuff.

www.makezine.com
Make Magazine's online version with forums, projects, a store, and blogs.